W9-CPC-331

f&w

cocktails 2010

FOOD&WINE

AMERICAN EXPRESS PUBLISHING CORPORATION, NEW YORK

FOOD & WINE COCKTAILS 2010

EDITOR **Kate Krader**
DEPUTY EDITORS **Jim Meehan, Joaquin Simo**
SENIOR EDITOR **Colleen McKinney**
COPY EDITOR **Lisa Leventer**
RESEARCHER **Janice Huang**
EDITORIAL ASSISTANT **Yasmin Fahr**

DESIGN DIRECTOR **Patricia Sanchez, Nice Kern, LLC**
PRODUCTION MANAGER **Matt Carson**
PARTY-FOOD RECIPE TESTER
Melissa Rubel Jacobson

PHOTOGRAPHER **Tina Rupp**
FOOD STYLIST **Alison Attenborough**
STYLE EDITOR **Jessica Romm**
ASSISTANT STYLIST **Eugenia Santiesteban**

ON THE COVER **Delta, P. 75**

AMERICAN EXPRESS PUBLISHING CORPORATION

PRESIDENT/C.E.O. **Ed Kelly**
S.V.P./CHIEF MARKETING OFFICER **Mark V. Stanich**
C.F.O./S.V.P./CORPORATE DEVELOPMENT &
OPERATIONS **Paul B. Francis**
V.P./GENERAL MANAGERS **Frank Bland,
Keith Strohmeier**

V.P., BOOKS & PRODUCTS/PUBLISHER
Marshall Corey
DIRECTOR, BOOK PROGRAMS **Bruce Spanier**
SENIOR MARKETING MANAGER, BRANDED BOOKS
Eric Lucie
ASSISTANT MARKETING MANAGER **Lizabeth Clark**
DIRECTOR OF FULFILLMENT & PREMIUM VALUE
Phil Black
MANAGER OF CUSTOMER EXPERIENCE &
PRODUCT DEVELOPMENT **Charles Graver**
DIRECTOR OF FINANCE **Thomas Noonan**
ASSOCIATE BUSINESS MANAGER **Uma Mahabir**
OPERATIONS DIRECTOR (PREPRESS)
Rosalie Abatemarco Samat
OPERATIONS DIRECTOR (MANUFACTURING)
Anthony White

ISBN 978-1-60320-837-6
ISSN 1554-4354

FOOD & WINE MAGAZINE

S.V.P./EDITOR IN CHIEF **Dana Cowin**
CREATIVE DIRECTOR **Stephen Scoble**
MANAGING EDITOR **Mary Ellen Ward**
EXECUTIVE EDITOR **Pamela Kaufman**
EXECUTIVE FOOD EDITOR **Tina Ujlaki**
EXECUTIVE ONLINE EDITOR **Rebecca Bauer**

FEATURES
FEATURES EDITOR **Michelle Shih**
RESTAURANT EDITOR **Kate Krader**
SENIOR EDITOR **Christine Quinlan**
SENIOR ONLINE EDITORS **Ratha Tep,
Tracy Ziemer**
TRAVEL EDITOR **Jen Murphy**
STYLE EDITOR **Jessica Romm**
ASSISTANT EDITORS **Alessandra Bulow,
Kerianne Hansen, Kelly Snowden**

FOOD
SENIOR EDITOR **Kate Heddings**
ASSOCIATE EDITORS **Kristin Donnelly,
Emily Kaiser**
TEST KITCHEN SUPERVISOR **Marcia Kiesel**
SENIOR RECIPE DEVELOPER **Grace Parisi**
SENIOR ASSOCIATE RECIPE DEVELOPER
Melissa Rubel Jacobson
KITCHEN ASSISTANT **Brian Malik**

WINE
WINE EDITOR **Ray Isle**
ASSISTANT EDITOR **Megan Krigbaum**

ART
ART DIRECTOR **Courtney Waddell Eckersley**
SENIOR DESIGNER **Michael Patti**
DESIGNER **James Maikowski**

PHOTO
DIRECTOR OF PHOTOGRAPHY **Fredrika Stjärne**
DEPUTY PHOTO EDITOR **Anthony LaSala**
PHOTO ASSISTANT **Rebecca Stepler**

PRODUCTION
PRODUCTION MANAGER **Matt Carson**
DESIGN/PRODUCTION ASSISTANT **Carl Hesler**

COPY & RESEARCH
COPY CHIEF **Michele Berkover Petry**
SENIOR COPY EDITOR **Ann Lien**
ASSISTANT RESEARCH EDITORS **John Mantia,
Emily McKenna**

Published by
American Express Publishing Corporation
1120 Avenue of the Americas, New York, NY 10036

Manufactured in the United States of America

cocktails 2010

FOOD&WINE
BOOKS

contents

La Joie, P. 126

"Silver Band" Champagne tulip by Dorothy C. Thorpe from Replacements, Ltd.; "Lulu" decanter by William Yeoward.

the entire planet, it seems, has become drink-obsessed. So we shifted the focus of our annual *F&W Cocktails* guide from the United States to the entire world.

With help from outstanding deputy editors Jim Meehan and Joaquin Simo (both star mixologists in their own right), we found talents like Hidetsugu Ueno at Tokyo's Bar High Five—a classics master who employs seven different shaking techniques when he mixes his drinks and stores his spirits at various temperatures to change their texture. We also noticed some excellent trends (don't just drop a mint leaf into a drink—smack it first). And we sought out terrific cocktail-friendly dishes like mini *croque-monsieurs* from Bar Meurice in Paris; they pair beautifully with the sherry-spiked Andalusian from Las Vegas mixologist Francesco Lafranconi. Turn the page to turn your house into one of the world's best cocktail bars.

DANA COWIN
EDITOR IN CHIEF
FOOD & WINE MAGAZINE

KATE KRADER
EDITOR
FOOD & WINE COCKTAILS 2010

Wheat and Barley, P. 120

"Drift Ice" double old-fashioned glass by Moser.

cocktail clinic

glassware arsenal

1 COUPE
A shallow, wide-mouthed glass primarily for small (a.k.a. short) and potent cocktails.

2 TIKI MUG
A ceramic mug without a handle that's decorated in a tropical or Polynesian-style motif. It's used for serving tiki drinks.

3 PILSNER
A flared glass designed for beer. It's also good for oversize cocktails or drinks with multiple garnishes.

4 COLLINS
A very tall, narrow glass often used for drinks served on ice and topped with soda.

5 WINEGLASS
A tall, slightly rounded, stemmed glass for wine-based cocktails. White wine glasses are a fine substitute for highball glasses and are also good for frozen drinks. Balloon-shaped red wine glasses are ideal for fruity cocktails as well as punches.

10

6 HIGHBALL
A tall, narrow glass that helps preserve the fizz in drinks served with ice and topped with soda.

7 SNIFTER
A wide-bowled glass for warm drinks, cocktails on ice and spirits served neat.

8 MARTINI
A stemmed glass with a cone-shaped bowl for cocktails that are served straight up (drinks that are chilled with ice before they're strained).

9 FIZZ
A narrow glass for soda-topped drinks without ice. Also called a Delmonico or juice glass.

10 FLUTE
A tall, slender, usually stemmed glass; its narrow shape helps keep cocktails that are topped with Champagne or sparkling wine effervescent.

11 ROCKS
A short, wide-mouthed glass for spirits served neat and cocktails poured over ice.

12 PINT
A large, flared 16-ounce glass, ideally made of tempered glass, used for stirring or shaking drinks, or for serving oversize cocktails with ice.

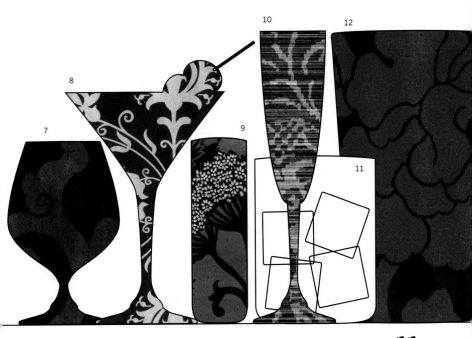

home bar tools

1 BOSTON SHAKER
The bartender's choice, consisting of a pint glass with a metal canister that covers the top of the glass to create a seal. Measure ingredients into the glass and shake with the metal half pointing away from you.

2 MUDDLER
A sturdy tool that's used to crush herbs, sugar cubes and fresh fruit; it's traditionally made of wood. Choose a muddler that can reach the bottom of a cocktail shaker; in a pinch, substitute a long-handled wooden spoon.

3 JULEP STRAINER
The preferred device for straining cocktails from a pint glass because it fits securely. Fine holes keep ice out of the drink.

4 CHANNEL KNIFE
A small, spoon-shaped knife with a metal tooth. Creates garnishes by turning citrus-fruit peels into long, thin twists.

5 WAITER'S CORKSCREW
A pocketknife-like tool with a bottle opener and a blade for cutting foil from wine caps. Bartenders prefer it to bulkier, more complicated corkscrews.

12

6 JIGGER
A two-sided stainless steel measuring instrument for precise mixing. Look for one with ½- and 1-ounce cups. A shot glass with measurements works well, too.

7 ICE PICK
A sharp metal tool with a sturdy handle used to break off chunks of ice from a larger block of ice.

8 BAR SPOON
A long-handled metal spoon that mixes cocktails without creating air bubbles. Also useful for measuring small amounts of liquid.

9 COBBLER SHAKER
The most commonly used shaker, with a metal cup for mixing drinks with ice, a built-in strainer and a fitted top.

10 CITRUS JUICER
A shallow dish with a reaming cone, a spout and often a strainer that's used to separate juice from pulp.

11 HAWTHORNE STRAINER
The best all-purpose strainer. A semicircular spring ensures a spill-proof fit on a shaker. Look for a tightly coiled spring, which keeps muddled fruit and herbs out of drinks.

mixology basics

making a twist

A twist—a small piece of citrus zest—adds concentrated citrus flavor from the peel's essential oils.

To make and use a standard twist
1 Use a sharp paring knife or vegetable peeler to cut a thin, oval, quarter-size disk of the peel, avoiding the pith (the white spongy part).
2 Gently grasp the outer edges skin side down between the thumb and two fingers and pinch the twist over the drink.
3 Rub the peel around the rim of the glass, then drop it into the drink.

To make a spiral-cut twist
1 Use a channel knife to cut a 3-inch-long piece of peel with some of the pith intact (this helps the spiral hold its shape). It's best to cut the twist over the glass so the essential oils from the peel fall into the drink.
2 Wrap the twist around a chopstick and tighten at both ends to create a curlicue shape.

flaming a twist

Flaming a lemon or orange twist caramelizes the zest's essential oils.

1 Cut a thin, oval, quarter-size piece of peel with a bit of the pith intact.
2 Gently grasp the outer edges skin side down between the thumb and two fingers and hold the twist about 4 inches over the cocktail.
3 Hold a lit match over the drink an inch away from the twist—don't let the flame touch the peel—then pinch the edges of the twist sharply so that the citrus oil falls through the flame and into the drink.

double straining

Drinks made with muddled fruit and herbs are sometimes double strained to remove tiny particles, so the cocktail is pristine and clear.

1 Place a very fine tea strainer over the serving glass.
2 Make the drink in a shaker, then set a Hawthorne strainer over the shaker and pour the drink through both strainers into the glass.

14

rimming a glass

Bartenders often coat only half of the rim of a glass so there's a choice of sides to sip from.

1 Spread a few tablespoonfuls of salt (preferably kosher), sugar or other powdered or very finely crushed ingredient on a small plate.
2 Moisten the outer rim of the glass with a citrus-fruit wedge, water or a syrup or colorful liquid like pomegranate juice. Then roll the outer rim of the glass on the plate until lightly coated.
3 Hold the glass upside down and tap to release any excess.

perfecting ice

Ice is key to a great drink. For serving most drinks, the bigger the pieces, the better. Large chunks of ice melt more slowly, and dilute drinks less. Detail-obsessed bars like Heaven's Dog in San Francisco cut ice from large blocks; Brooklyn's Clover Club uses molds to make ice cylinders that just fit inside a rocks glass. The exception to the big-ice rule: the crushed ice in juleps and swizzled drinks. Besides melting quickly, which dilutes potent drinks, crushed ice also adds an appealing frost to glasses. Cracked ice is used principally for stirring. It helps to cool down a drink more quickly than stirring with standard-size ice cubes.

To make big blocks of ice for punch bowls, pour water into a large, shallow plastic container and freeze. To unmold, first warm the bottom of the container in hot water.

To make extra-large ice cubes for rocks glasses, simply use a slightly smaller glass as a mold. To unmold, run warm water over the outside of the glass to slide the ice cube out. Or make a large block of ice in a loaf pan and use an ice pick to break off chunks the size you want.

To make crushed ice, cover cubes in a clean kitchen towel and pound with a hammer or rolling pin.

To make cracked ice, place a square ice cube in the palm of your hand and tap it three times with the back of a bar spoon, tapping a different side of the cube each time.

To make completely clear cubes, fill ice trays with hot filtered water.

To make perfectly square cubes, use flexible silicone Perfect Cube ice trays (available from surlatable.com).

homemade mixers

simple syrup

This bar staple is one of the most universal mixers, essential to many well-balanced cocktails. Stash a jar of the syrup in your refrigerator; it keeps for up to 1 month.

MAKES ABOUT 12 OUNCES
In a small saucepan, combine 1 cup water and 1 cup sugar. Bring the mixture to a boil over moderately high heat, stirring to dissolve the sugar, about 3 minutes. Let cool, then transfer the syrup to a jar, cover and refrigerate until ready to use.

rich simple syrup

Using demerara sugar gives this concentrated syrup a great molasses flavor. The syrup keeps for up to 1 month in the fridge.

MAKES ABOUT 8 OUNCES
In a small saucepan, combine 1 cup demerara sugar and ½ cup water. Bring to a boil over moderately high heat, stirring to dissolve the sugar, about 3 minutes. Let cool, transfer to a jar, cover and refrigerate.

easiest simple syrup

This extremely easy way to make simple syrup without a stove or saucepan is an old bartender's trick. The syrup keeps for up to 1 month in the fridge.

MAKES ABOUT 12 OUNCES
In a bottle or jar with a tight-fitting lid, combine 1 cup superfine sugar with 1 cup hot water and shake hard. Refrigerate until ready to use.

A WORD ON
honey and agave

Mixologists are increasingly using natural sweeteners like honey and agave nectar in place of simple syrup because they impart a more complex flavor to drinks. To make a pourable syrup, warm the honey or agave nectar over low heat before mixing it with an equal part of water. Or simply put equal parts of the sweetener and warm water in a jar and shake well to combine. For a richer syrup, use twice as much sweetener as water. Let the syrup come to room temperature before using it in drinks.

conversion charts

CUPS	OUNCES	LITERS
4¼ CUPS	34 OUNCES	1 LITER
4 CUPS	32 OUNCES	
3 CUPS	24 OUNCES	
2 CUPS	16 OUNCES	
1 CUP	8 OUNCES	
¾ CUP	6 OUNCES	
½ CUP	4 OUNCES	
¼ CUP	2 OUNCES	60 MILLILITERS

TABLESPOONS	OUNCES	MILLILITERS
2 TABLESPOONS	1 OUNCE	30 MILLILITERS
1½ TABLESPOONS	¾ OUNCE	
4 TEASPOONS	$^2/_3$ OUNCE	20 MILLILITERS
1 TABLESPOON	½ OUNCE	15 MILLILITERS
2 TEASPOONS	$^1/_3$ OUNCE	10 MILLILITERS
1½ TEASPOONS	¼ OUNCE	

essential spirits

Mixologists are using more and more esoteric spirits in their drinks, but these five choices are still the backbone of a great cocktail list.

gin

A dry, clear spirit, gin is distilled with many botanicals, such as juniper, coriander, cardamom and dried citrus peel. These ingredients often add piney, spicy or citrusy notes. Ubiquitous dry gin, also known as **London dry,** is bolder in flavor than the slightly sweet, less botanically intense **Old Tom** style.

vodka

Produced all over the world, vodka is traditionally distilled from fermented grain or potatoes, but nearly any fruit or vegetable that contains starch or sugar can be used, from grapes to beets. The finest flavored vodkas are often made with fruit-infused grain alcohol that's run through a pot still.

18

tequila

The best examples of this agave-based spirit are made with 100 percent blue agave. **Blanco** tequila is aged for up to two months. **Reposado** ("rested") tequila sits for up to a year. **Añejo** ("aged") tequila ages for up to three years. **Extra añejo** tequila ages for a minimum of three years. **Mezcal,** also agave-based, is smokier than tequila. Artisanally produced versions from Oaxaca are becoming more popular.

whiskey

This spirit is distilled from a fermented mash of grains and aged in wood barrels. (Whiskey is spelled without an "e" in Scotland and Canada.) **Scotch** whisky is made in two major styles: **single-malt** whisky, which is made from 100 percent malted barley and pot-distilled from one distillery; and **blended** whisky, a mixture of single-malt and grain whisky from more than one distillery. The smoky flavor in some Scotches comes from drying malted barley with peat smoke.

rum

Distilled from cane syrup, molasses or fresh pressed sugarcane, rums are primarily produced in tropical regions. **White** rums typically age for a short time in wood. **Amber,** or gold, rums usually age in oak barrels. **Dark** rums, especially Jamaican ones, tend to be rich and flavorful. **Rhum agricole** is made in the French West Indies from fresh pressed sugarcane juice (not syrup or molasses).

spirits lexicon

Absinthe An anise-flavored spirit formerly banned in the United States. It's flavored with such botanicals as wormwood, green anise and fennel seeds.

Agave nectar A thin, sweet syrup made from the sap of the cactus-like agave plant.

Amaro A bittersweet Italian herbal liqueur often served as an after-dinner drink. Grappa-based **Nardini amaro** is flavored with bitter orange, peppermint and gentian.

Aperol A bittersweet Italian aperitif flavored with bitter orange, rhubarb and gentian.

Apple brandy A distilled fermented apple cider that is aged in oak barrels. Most of the brandy is bottled at 80 proof, but **bonded apple brandy,** which is preferable in cocktails

because of its concentrated green-apple flavor, is 100 proof.

Applejack An American apple brandy often blended with neutral spirits.

Aquavit A clear, grain- or potato-based Scandinavian spirit flavored with caraway seeds and other botanicals, such as fennel, anise and citrus peel.

Barolo Chinato An Italian digestif made from Nebbiolo-based wine (produced in Piedmont's Barolo zone) and various herbs and spices, including cardamom, rhubarb and quinine (*china*).

Bénédictine A brandy-based herbal liqueur derived from a recipe developed by a French monk in 1510.

Bitters A concentrated tincture of bitter and aromatic herbs, roots and spices that adds flavor and complexity to drinks. Varieties include orange, chocolate, rhubarb and aromatic bitters, the best known of which is **Angostura,** created in Angostura, Venezuela, in 1824. **Fee Brothers bitters,** which come in 10 flavors, have been made in Rochester, New York, for more than 60 years. (See also **Peychaud's bitters.**)

20

Calvados A cask-aged brandy made in the Normandy region of France from apples and sometimes pears.

Campari A potent, bitter, bright red Italian aperitif made from fruit, herbs and aromatics.

Carpano Antica Formula A rich and complex crimson-colored sweet Italian vermouth.

Chartreuse A spicy French herbal liqueur made from more than 100 botanicals; **green** Chartreuse is more potent than the honey-sweetened **yellow** one.

Cognac An oak-aged brandy made from grapes grown in the Charente region of France. **VSOP** (Very Superior Old Pale) Cognac must be aged a minimum of four years in French oak barrels.

Cointreau A French triple sec that is made by macerating and distilling sun-dried sweet and bitter orange peels.

Curaçao A general term for orange-flavored liqueurs produced in the Dutch West Indies.

Cynar A pleasantly bitter Italian liqueur made from 13 herbs and plants, including artichokes.

Dimmi A fruity and floral liqueur infused with licorice, vanilla, bitter orange and peach.

Dubonnet A wine-based, quinine-enhanced aperitif that comes in two varieties. The **rouge** is full-bodied. The drier **blanc** is a good substitute for dry vermouth.

Eau-de-vie A clear, unaged fruit brandy. Classic varieties include **framboise** (raspberry), **poire** (pear), **abricot** (apricot), **kirsch** (cherry) and **mirabelle** (plum).

Fernet-Branca A potent, bitter Italian digestif made from 27 herbs.

Galliano A golden Italian liqueur made with some 30 herbs and spices, including lavender, anise, juniper and vanilla.

Genever A clear, botanically rich, malted grain–based spirit from Holland. **Oude** refers to the maltier old-style; lighter, less malty versions are called **jonge.**

Grenadine A sweet red syrup made from pomegranate juice and sugar (see the Homemade Grenadine recipe on P. 118).

Heering cherry liqueur A Danish brandy-based cherry liqueur.

Herbsaint An anise-flavored absinthe substitute produced in New Orleans.

Kümmel A grain-based liqueur first distilled in Holland in the late 1500s. It's flavored with cumin, caraway and fennel.

Licor 43 A citrus-and-vanilla-flavored Spanish liqueur made from a combination of 43 herbs and spices.

Lillet A wine-based French aperitif flavored with orange peel and quinine. The lesser-known **rouge** variety is sweeter than the more widely available **blanc.**

Limoncello An Italian liqueur that's made from lemon peels soaked in neutral spirits and then sweetened with sugar.

Madeira A fortified wine from the island of Madeira, usually named for one of four grape varieties: **Sercial** (the driest), **Verdelho, Bual** or **Malmsey,** which are progressively sweeter.

Maraschino liqueur A clear Italian liqueur, the best of which is distilled from bittersweet marasca cherries and their pits, aged in ash barrels, then sweetened with sugar.

Marsala A Sicilian fortified wine; styles include **secco** (dry), often served as an aperitif, and **semisecco** (semisweet) and **dolce** (sweet), commonly served as dessert wines.

Mezcal An agave-based spirit with a smoky flavor that comes from roasting the agave hearts in earthen pits before fermentation. The finest mezcal is made in Mexico's Oaxaca region.

Navan A Cognac-based liqueur infused with Madagascar vanilla.

Noilly Prat rouge A bittersweet red vermouth from the south of France made from a secret mixture of herbs and spices, including saffron, quinine and cloves.

Pernod A French producer of a liqueur made from the essential oils of star anise and fennel combined with herbs, spices, sugar and a neutral spirit. Pernod recently rereleased their absinthe, which, like all absinthes, had been banned in the U.S. since 1912.

Peychaud's bitters
A brand of bitters with bright anise and cranberry flavors; the recipe dates to 19th-century New Orleans.

Pimm's No. 1 A gin-based English aperitif often served with ginger beer or lemonade.

Pineau des Charentes A barrel-aged French aperitif produced from unfermented grape juice and young Cognac.

Pisco A clear brandy distilled from grapes in the wine-producing regions of Peru and Chile.

Poire Williams A pear eau-de-vie, usually made in Switzerland or the Alsace region of France.

Port A fortified wine from the Douro region of Portugal. Styles include fruity, young **ruby** ports; richer, nuttier **tawnies;** thick-textured, oak-aged **late bottled vintage** (LBV) versions; and decadent **vintage** ports, made from the best grapes in the best vintages. Dry **white** port is often served chilled, as an aperitif.

Punt e Mes A spicy, orange-accented sweet vermouth fortified with bitters.

Sherry A fortified wine from Spain's Jerez region. Varieties include dry styles like **fino** and **manzanilla;** nuttier, richer **amontillados** and **olorosos;** and viscous sweet versions such as **Pedro Ximénez** (PX) and **cream sherry.**

Sloe gin A bittersweet liqueur produced by infusing gin or a neutral spirit with sloe berries and sugar.

St. Elizabeth Allspice Dram An Austrian rum-based liqueur made with Jamaican allspice berries.

St-Germain elderflower liqueur A French liqueur made by blending macerated elderflower blossoms with eau-de-vie. It has hints of pear, peach and grapefruit zest.

Strega A bittersweet Italian liqueur infused with about 70 herbs and spices, including saffron, which gives it a golden yellow color.

Triple sec An orange-flavored liqueur that is similar to curaçao but not as sweet. Cointreau is the most famous, created in France in 1875.

Velvet Falernum A low-alcohol, sugarcane-based liqueur from Barbados flavored with clove, almond and lime.

Vermouth An aromatic fortified wine. The dry **white** variety is used in martinis. **Sweet** vermouth, which is usually red, is often used for Manhattans. **Bianco** vermouth is an aromatic, sweet white vermouth traditionally served on the rocks.

10 international drink trends

1 bespoke glassware

At many bars, glasses have become as one-of-a-kind as the cocktails in them. Acclaimed Danish designer Cecilie Manz created special flutes and wineglasses for Copenhagen's Nimb hotel bar (their shapes were inspired by the tulips in the city's Tivoli Gardens). And the Artesian bar in London's Langham Hotel uses glasses designed by John Jenkins, including a Victorian seltzer glass and a "fat cocktail" glass that holds a pint of liquid.

2 drinks as herb gardens

For plenty of mixologists, the more herb sprigs in a drink, the better (extra credit for using micro-herbs, or for growing herbs at the bar, as Adam Seger does at Chicago's Nacional 27). Bartenders are also "smacking" herbs: slapping them between their palms over a drink to release essential oils—and, of course, to add drama to the spectator experience. (Angus Winchester smacks a mint sprig over his Gone Native, P. 74.)

3 super-spicy cocktails

The newest ingredients in cocktails: chiles. That means fresh chiles muddled into a drink or added as a garnish, a sprinkle of cayenne pepper and even chile pastes and hot sauces mixed into cocktails, such as the Indonesian *sambal oelek* that's stirred into the Wild Colonial (P. 66).

4 colder-than-ice spirits

Elite mixologists like Hidetsugu Ueno of Tokyo's Bar High Five (P. 28) use spirits at different temperatures—sometimes colder than ice, sometimes not—to change the viscosity of the drink and add texture. Accordingly, some new bar refrigerators have a range of below-freezing zones.

5 new rising-star spirits

Genever, a centuries-old Dutch spirit, is replacing vodka in drinks like the Vanilla-Berry Crush (P. 67). Bartenders are sourcing more sophisticated mezcals, tequila's smoky cousin, as distilleries buy agave from remote regions of Mexico. Mezcal is a frequent substitute for tequila in cocktails

24

like the Maguey Sour (P. 94). And boutique distilleries are making small-batch pisco, Peru's national spirit; mixologist Hans Hilburg of El Pisquerito in Cuzco highlights it in his Cholo Fresco (P. 152).

6 tiki's comeback

Tiki is back, and bartenders are taking it seriously, sourcing excellent rums from specific Caribbean islands and South American countries. Jeff Berry, who has chronicled tiki trends for nearly two decades, includes several outstanding tiki recipes (like the Kon-Tini, P. 101) in the Rum chapter.

7 avant-garde bar tools

Mixologists are adding ever more unconventional tools to their bar arsenals. They're using atomizers filled with bitters or an intense spirit to flavor a glass or garnish a drink (as in the Alejandro, P. 76) and cream whippers and nitrous oxide chargers to create flavored foams for topping drinks (like the sweet blueberry foam on the Wormwood Candy, P. 64).

8 bitters in any flavor

In the last few years, the array of exotically flavored bitters (super-concentrated solutions that flavor drinks) has exploded. Look for more drinks with celery bitters or even the once-elusive Bittermens Xocolatl Mole Bitters (bittermens.com). Bars such as Melbourne's Der Raum even make versions of 19th-century bitters, like the cardamom-spiked Boker's.

9 micro-batch mixers

Drink specialists don't make syrups and bitters just for their own drinks anymore; they're selling them to the public. Jennifer Colliau of the Slanted Door in San Francisco offers her terrific orgeat (almond-flavored syrup) at smallhandfoods.com.

10 the return of liqueurs

With the renewed interest in old-school spirits like pimento dram (the rum-based St. Elizabeth Allspice Dram is a new version of it), mixologists are rediscovering liqueurs. These range from the now-ubiquitous St-Germain elderflower liqueur to fruit-flavored ones, like apricot.

classics

LEFT TO RIGHT Negroni, P. 29; Cuba Libre, P. 34; Sidecar, P. 36

Details, left to right: "Palatin" rocks glass by Theresienthal; "Vertical Strait" highball glass by Calvin Klein; "Mr. Egg" Champagne saucer by Květná from TableArt.

HIDETSUGU UENO

Tokyo is full of bartenders obsessed with classic cocktails, but Bar High Five's Hidetsugu Ueno is widely regarded as the best. The meticulous craftsman not only carves ice cubes to look like jewels but keeps spirits at various temperatures—sometimes even checking finished cocktails with a thermometer—to make his impeccable, invariably dry drinks. These range from well-known cocktails like Manhattans (p. 36) to more obscure ones like the apricot-accented Czarine (p. 30).

classics

■ negroni

Ice
1⅓ ounces frozen gin,
     preferably London dry
  1 ounce sweet vermouth
 ⅔ ounce Campari
  1 orange wheel,
     for garnish

Ueno currently uses the exquisite French Dolin rouge vermouth in his Negronis, but you may want to experiment with different sweet vermouths—Martini & Rossi, Cinzano, Carpano Antica Formula—or try a bittersweet one like Punt e Mes.

Fill a rocks glass with ice. Add the gin, vermouth and Campari and stir well. Garnish with the orange wheel.

■ rebujito

Ice
1½ ounces fino sherry,
     preferably Tio Pepe
  3 ounces chilled Sprite

This low-alcohol spritzer is thought to have originated in Andalucía, but versions of it exist all over Spain. Some people replace the dry, nutty fino sherry with slightly floral manzanilla; others use tonic or soda water and fresh lemon juice instead of Sprite.

Fill a highball glass with ice. Add the sherry and Sprite and stir gently.

▮ kamikaze

Ice
1½ ounces vodka
2 teaspoons Cointreau
or other triple sec
½ ounce fresh lime juice

Although its name is often associated with high-octane shots and happy-hour specials, this drink is a classic. Some historians trace its origins to a bar on the American naval base in Yokosuka, Japan, during the late 1940s or early '50s.

Fill a cocktail shaker with ice. Add the vodka, Cointreau and lime juice and shake well. Strain into an ice-filled rocks glass.

 czarine

Cracked ice
1½ ounces frozen vodka
½ ounce dry vermouth
2½ teaspoons apricot
liqueur
Dash of Angostura bitters

To keep this drink from getting too cold, Ueno employs what he calls a low-speed stir. "You have to feel when the stir gets heavy," he says. "That's the moment when the apricot aroma really comes through."

Fill a pint glass with cracked ice. Add all of the remaining ingredients and stir well. Strain the drink into a chilled coupe.

Czarine

*"Darling Point" Champagne
glasses by Kate Spade for Lenox.*

♆ margarita

1 lime wedge and kosher salt
Ice
2 ounces blanco tequila
½ ounce Cointreau or other triple sec
¾ ounce fresh lime juice

There are many stories associated with the margarita's origins. The prevailing one credits Texas socialite Margaret Sames, who combined the ingredients in salt-rimmed glasses with the Spanish version of her name etched on them.

Moisten half of the outer rim of a chilled coupe with the lime wedge and coat lightly with salt. Fill a cocktail shaker with ice. Add the tequila, Cointreau and lime juice and shake well. Strain the drink into the prepared glass.

■ matador

Ice
1½ ounces blanco tequila
1 ounce unsweetened pineapple juice
⅓ ounce fresh lime juice

Ueno chooses from seven different shaking methods when making his cocktails: hard, high-speed, short-pitch, long-stroke, regular two-step, regular three-step or non-step. For matadors he uses the short-pitch shake, which involves the wrist only; it adds air and "whips" the drink.

Fill a cocktail shaker with ice. Add the tequila, pineapple juice and lime juice and shake well. Strain the drink into an ice-filled rocks glass.

32

classics

♆ daiquiri

MAKES 8 DRINKS

Ice
- 16 ounces white rum
- 5 ounces fresh lime juice
- 2 ounces Brown Sugar Syrup (below)

Use any leftover Brown Sugar Syrup to sweeten old-fashioneds or Sazeracs or as a topping for pancakes, waffles or ice cream.

Fill a large cocktail shaker with ice. Add the rum, lime juice and Brown Sugar Syrup and shake well. Strain the drink into chilled coupes.

BROWN SUGAR SYRUP

In a small saucepan, bring ²/₃ cup water and 1 cup light brown sugar to a boil; simmer over moderate heat, stirring, until the sugar is dissolved, about 3 minutes. Remove from the heat and let cool completely, then pour into a jar, cover and refrigerate for up to 1 month. Makes about 10 ounces.

cuba libre

Ice
1½ ounces white rum
3 ounces chilled
Coca-Cola
1 teaspoon fresh
lime juice
1 lime wedge,
for garnish

The best kind of cola to use in this drink is Mexican Coca-Cola (available at amazon.com) or another brand made with cane sugar. Sugar-based colas have a crisper, cleaner flavor than the more readily available ones made with high-fructose corn syrup.

Fill a highball glass with ice. Add the rum, Coca-Cola and lime juice and stir gently. Garnish with the lime wedge.

 # harvard cooler

Ice
1½ ounces Calvados
⅓ ounce fresh lemon
juice
1 teaspoon Simple
Syrup (P. 16)
1½ ounces chilled
club soda

According to Ueno, this somewhat obscure, apple-accented cocktail is extremely popular in Japanese bars. Some people omit the club soda and call it a Moonlight.

Fill a cocktail shaker with ice. Add the Calvados, lemon juice and Simple Syrup and shake well. Strain into an ice-filled highball glass, then stir in the club soda.

34

Harvard Cooler

*"TAC 02" highball
glass by Rosenthal.*

▼ sidecar

Ice
1½ ounces chilled VSOP
     Cognac
 ½ ounce Grand Marnier
 ⅓ ounce fresh lemon juice

Robert Vermeire's 1922 book Cocktails: How to Mix Them *attributes the sidecar to the celebrated bartender MacGarry, who worked at London's Buck's Club.*

Fill a cocktail shaker with ice. Add the Cognac, Grand Marnier and lemon juice and shake well. Double strain (p. 14) the drink into a chilled coupe.

▼ manhattan

Cracked ice
1½ ounces frozen
     overproof bourbon
 ½ ounce sweet vermouth
 ½ teaspoon Carpano
     Antica Formula
     (sweet Italian
     vermouth)
  1 maraschino cherry,
     for garnish

At Bar High Five, Ueno stores spirits at various temperatures to ensure the optimum texture and temperature of each drink. He keeps the bourbon for his Manhattans at −4 degrees Fahrenheit. (You can achieve a similar effect by chilling bourbon in the freezer for a day.)

Fill a pint glass with cracked ice. Add the bourbon, vermouth and Carpano Antica Formula and stir well. Strain into a chilled coupe and garnish with the cherry.

36

classics

▼ hunter

Cracked ice
1½ ounces overproof
    bourbon
½ ounce cherry Heering
    (cherry liqueur)

This potent drink is terrific for warming up after a day of skiing (or hunting).

Fill a pint glass with cracked ice. Add the bourbon and cherry Heering and stir well. Strain the drink into a chilled coupe.

▼ grasshopper

Ice
1 ounce white crème
    de cacao
1 ounce crème de
    menthe
1 ounce heavy cream

Cocktail historians credit this minty concoction to Philibert Guichet, former owner of Tujague's Restaurant in New Orleans. Guichet entered the recipe in a New York City cocktail contest in 1919, just before Prohibition began. The drink won second prize.

Fill a cocktail shaker with ice. Add the crème de cacao, crème de menthe and cream and shake well. Double strain (p. 14) the drink into a chilled coupe.

aperitifs

LEFT TO RIGHT Cinque Terre, P. 41; Sorrentino, P. 45

Details, left to right: "Pitagora" highball glass by Marco Zanuso for Arnolfo di Cambio from Moss; "Kikatsu" old-fashioned glass from Eastern Accent.

FRANCESCO LAFRANCONI

Francesco Lafranconi has a preternatural knack for creating exceptional aperitifs; that's probably because before-dinner drinks are a custom in his native Italy. The Las Vegas–based director of mixology for the megadistributor Southern Wine & Spirits, Lafranconi thinks like a chef when devising his recipes, playing up a spirit's botanical flavors with straightforward ingredients (grapefruit) and offbeat ones (Cape gooseberry jam). And like many chefs, he enjoys pairing food and drinks. His favorite combination is the Cortés (p. 46) with seared foie gras.

"EX LIBRIS" WALLPAPER BY
PIERO FORNASETTI FROM COLE & SON.

aperitifs

▮ cinque terre

5 medium lemon verbena
    sprigs, plus 1 lemon
    verbena sprig and
    3 leaves for garnish
1 strip of orange zest
1 strip of lemon zest
Ice
2 ounces bianco vermouth
    (sweet white vermouth)
2 ounces chilled Prosecco
¼ ounce green Chartreuse

This bubbly, citrusy drink is named after the famous cluster of five villages perched on a stretch of cliffs on the northwest coast of Italy.

In a collins glass, lightly muddle the 5 lemon verbena sprigs with the orange and lemon zests. Add ice and the vermouth and Prosecco and stir well. Top with the Chartreuse and garnish with the remaining verbena sprig and leaves.

♟ à tout à l'heure

½ ounce St-Germain
    elderflower liqueur
½ ounce pear eau-de-vie
½ ounce maraschino
    liqueur
½ ounce Verdelho-style
    Madeira
2 dashes of Angostura
    bitters
2 ounces chilled
    Champagne
1 lemon twist, for garnish

The first five ingredients for this drink can be combined and refrigerated in a glass jar or bottle indefinitely. Then, whenever you want a cocktail, all you need to do is add sparkling wine and a twist.

In a chilled pint glass, combine all of the ingredients except the Champagne and the garnish and stir well. Pour into a chilled flute. Top with the Champagne and garnish with the lemon twist.

pan americano

Ice
2 ounces chilled Sauvignon Blanc or other crisp white wine
¾ ounce pisco
¾ ounce Aperol (bitter orange Italian aperitif)
¾ ounce yellow Chartreuse
1 ounce chilled club soda
One 2-inch strip of Ruby Red grapefruit zest, for garnish

In a quest to create a drink using Peruvian pisco, Lafranconi ultimately settled on this unusual concoction. The Chartreuse-Aperol-grapefruit combination lingers for several minutes—an especially complex finish for an aperitif.

Fill a white wine glass with ice. Add all of the remaining ingredients except the garnish and stir well. Garnish with the grapefruit zest.

 # red velvet

2 ounces chilled framboise lambic
½ ounce crème de framboise (raspberry liqueur)
2 ounces chilled Prosecco
1 or 2 raspberries skewered on a rosemary sprig, for garnish

This riff on the Black Velvet replaces the Champagne with Prosecco and the Guinness with raspberry-flavored lambic, a type of wheat beer made with wild yeasts.

In a chilled pint glass, combine the lambic and crème de framboise and stir gently. Pour the drink into a chilled flute and top with the Prosecco. Garnish with the rosemary-skewered raspberries.

Red Velvet

"Cartoccio" flute by Carlo Moretti from TableArt.

▼ le monde

Ice

1½ ounces Bitter Orange
Vodka (below)
or orange vodka

½ ounce Pineau
des Charentes
(Cognac-fortified
grape juice)

½ ounce Aperol
(bitter orange Italian
aperitif)

½ ounce ginger liqueur

½ ounce chilled
sparkling wine

1 grapefruit twist,
for garnish

Bitter and aromatic gentian root—a key component of Angostura bitters, and here infused in orange vodka—is one of Lafranconi's favorite cocktail ingredients. It's sold at health-food stores.

Fill a pint glass with ice. Add all of the remaining ingredients except the garnish and stir well. Strain into a chilled coupe and garnish with the grapefruit twist.

BITTER ORANGE VODKA

In a jar, combine 1 tablespoon cut dried gentian root with 8 ounces orange vodka. Cover and let stand at room temperature for 24 hours. Strain the infused vodka into another jar, cover and refrigerate for up to 1 month. Makes about 8 ounces.

44

aperitifs

 ## andalusian

4 mint sprigs
2 dashes of peach bitters
Ice
2 ounces fino sherry
2 ounces chilled bitter
  lemon soda
One 2-inch strip of
  lemon zest

The Andalusian is perhaps the perfect brunch drink. Nutty, minty and light, it's based on a traditional aperitif served in Jerez, Spain, where sherry is produced.

In a white wine glass, gently muddle the mint sprigs with the peach bitters. Half fill the glass with ice, add the sherry and bitter lemon soda and stir well. Garnish with the lemon zest.

■ sorrentino

Ice
1 ounce Campari
1 ounce Barolo Chinato
  (spicy, wine-based
  digestif)
¾ ounce limoncello
1 ounce chilled club soda
1 thyme sprig, smacked
  (P. 24), and 1 lemon
  wheel and 1 orange
  wheel skewered on
  a pick, for garnish

If you can't find Barolo Chinato, use the spicy sweet vermouth Punt e Mes, which is widely available in the United States.

Fill a rocks glass with ice. Add all of the remaining ingredients except the garnishes and stir well. Garnish with the thyme sprig and the skewered lemon and orange wheels.

▼ cortés

2 ounces chilled late-harvest wine
1 ounce frozen reposado tequila, preferably Patrón
1 tangerine or grapefruit twist
3 prickly pear wedges skewered on a pick, for garnish (optional)

Reposado tequila, which typically ages for up to a year in wooden casks, gives this three-ingredient drink both a mellow oak taste and a lovely golden color.

In a chilled coupe or martini glass, combine the wine and tequila and stir gently. Pinch the tangerine twist over the drink, rub it around the rim of the glass and discard. Garnish with the prickly pear wedges.

▼ hour cocktail

Ice
1½ ounces gin
¾ ounce Dimmi (herbal Italian liqueur)
¾ ounce Lillet blanc
Dash of celery bitters
Dash of lemon bitters
1 tangerine or orange twist, for garnish

This amazingly clean and crisp drink is made with Dimmi, an organic wheat spirit infused with licorice, vanilla, bitter orange and rhubarb. Here it's mixed with celery and lemon bitters, available from cocktailkingdom.com.

Fill a pint glass with ice. Add all of the remaining ingredients except the garnish and stir well. Strain into a chilled coupe and garnish with the tangerine twist.

46

Cortés

"Verglas Platinum" cocktail glass by Roost; "Silver Band" pitcher by Dorothy C. Thorpe from Replacements, Ltd.

♟ mistral

1 orange twist
Ice
1½ ounces lemon vodka
½ ounce Dubonnet blanc
½ ounce Galliano
(Italian herbal liqueur)
½ ounce limoncello
2 dashes of Peychaud's
bitters
1 lemon twist and
1 thyme sprig,
for garnish

The bracing thyme, lemon and orange aromas in this drink remind Lafranconi of the mistral that blows through southern France, sending the scent of wild herbs and flowers across the countryside.

In a pint glass, muddle the orange twist. Add ice and all of the remaining ingredients except the lemon twist and thyme sprig and stir well. Strain the drink into a chilled coupe or martini glass and garnish with the lemon twist and thyme sprig.

48

Mistral

*"Ibex" cocktail
glass by Roost.*

☒ the man and the sea

Dash of absinthe

Ice

¾ ounce cucumber vodka

¾ ounce genever (P. 21)

1½ ounces chilled Clamato juice

½ ounce fresh lemon juice

Pinch each of salt and freshly ground pepper

Dash each of Worcestershire sauce and jalapeño hot sauce, more to taste

1 cucumber wheel and 1 dill sprig, for garnish

This is Lafranconi's elevated version of a Bloody Mary. For him, the briny mixture of cucumber, herbs and Clamato juice evokes the smell of salt water and seaweed at Fisherman's Wharf in San Francisco.

Rinse a chilled martini glass with the absinthe. Fill a pint glass with ice, then add all of the remaining ingredients except the garnishes and stir well. Strain the drink into the prepared martini glass and garnish with the cucumber wheel and dill sprig.

50

aperitifs

♈ forget-me-not

1 mint sprig
Ice
1 ounce gin, preferably
   Bombay Sapphire
1 ounce bonded apple
   brandy
½ ounce Punt e Mes
   (spicy sweet vermouth)
½ ounce Navan
   (vanilla-flavored
   Cognac-based liqueur)
2 dashes of orange bitters
1 brandied cherry,
   for garnish

According to Lafranconi, the botanicals in many aperitif ingredients (such as the gin, vermouth and bitters in this drink) are "eupeptic," meaning they stimulate taste receptors and the appetite.

Rub the inside of a chilled coupe with the mint sprig and discard. Fill a pint glass with ice, then add all of the remaining ingredients except the garnish and stir well. Strain into the prepared coupe and garnish with the cherry.

♈ the majestic

Ice
1½ ounces gin, preferably
   London dry
¾ ounce Grand Marnier
¾ ounce fresh lime juice
2 teaspoons Cape
   gooseberry jam
   or bitter orange
   marmalade
2 dashes of Angostura
   bitters
1 fresh kaffir lime leaf,
   for garnish (optional)

While visiting his friend Tim Rita, head bartender at Lewers Lounge in Honolulu's Halekulani hotel, Lafranconi came up with the idea to create a cocktail using the hotel's house-made poha berry (a.k.a. Cape gooseberry) jam.

Fill a cocktail shaker with ice. Add the gin, Grand Marnier, lime juice and jam and shake well. Strain the drink into a chilled coupe and add the bitters. Garnish with the lime leaf.

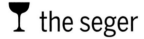 cynar sour

Ice
- 2 ounces Cynar
- ¼ ounce maraschino liqueur
- 1 ounce fresh lemon juice
- ¼ ounce agave nectar
- ½ large egg white (optional)
- 1 baby cucumber, halved and skewered on a pick (optional), and 3 long, thin strips of orange zest, for garnish

"Cynar is so distinctively Italian," *says Lafranconi about the bitter artichoke* *liqueur. "It has a very pleasing* *burnt-sugar, earthy, bittersweet flavor."*

Fill a cocktail shaker with ice. Add all of the remaining ingredients except the garnishes and shake well. Strain into a chilled coupe or snifter and garnish with the baby cucumber and orange zest.

the seger

- 3 dashes of Angostura bitters

Ice
- 1½ ounces blended Scotch
- ¾ ounce dry Marsala
- ¾ ounce Aperol (bitter orange Italian aperitif)
- ½ ounce fresh lemon juice
- Dash of orange flower water
- 1 orange twist
- 1 mint leaf, smacked (P. 24), for garnish

Lafranconi cleverly uses bitters to flavor *the glass before pouring in the cocktail.*

Rinse a chilled coupe with the bitters. Fill a cocktail shaker with ice. Add all of the remaining ingredients except the twist and the mint leaf. Shake well, then strain into the prepared coupe. Pinch the twist over the drink, rub it around the rim of the glass and discard. Garnish with the mint leaf.

Cynar Sour

"Etched Circles" wineglass by Calvin Klein.

LEFT TO RIGHT Incan, P. 60; The Wild Colonial, P. 66

*Details, left to right: "Newport" martini glass by
Theresienthal; "Stockholm" tumbler by Giarimi from Huset.*

vodka, aquavit & genever

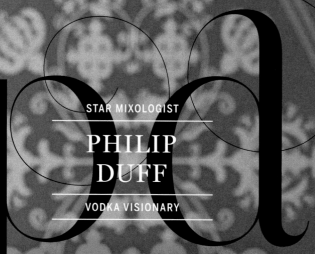

56

PHILIP DUFF

While some mixologists scorn vodka, Philip Duff is out to prove them wrong. "I like to get people drinking vodka in ways that highlight its unique flavors and styles," he says, pointing out, for example, the baked-bread and dried-fruit aromas of wheat-based Russian vodkas. "The same is true for northern European spirits like aquavit and genever." Duff made a name for himself at the outstanding speakeasy Door 74 in Amsterdam, and has earned such a reputation that one of his drinks, the genever-based Vanilla-Berry Crush (p. 67), is served at Amsterdam's Schiphol airport.

"STELLA" WALLPAPER BY MARCEL WANDERS
FOR GRAHAM & BROWN FROM DESIGN PUBLIC.

vodka,
aquavit & genever

■ ## russian cocktail

Crushed ice
2½ ounces vodka
1½ ounces cherry Heering
     (cherry liqueur)
  1 fresh black cherry
     skewered on a pick,
     for garnish

This potent recipe was adapted from one in the 1911 Beverages De Luxe, *edited by Geo. R. Washburne and Stanley Bronner. Many cocktail historians consider it the world's oldest vodka cocktail.*

Fill a rocks glass with crushed ice, then add the vodka and cherry Heering. Set a swizzle stick or bar spoon in the glass and spin it between your hands to mix the drink. Garnish with the skewered cherry.

 ## uncle vanya

Ice
  1 ounce vodka
  1 ounce crème de mûre
     (blackberry liqueur)
  2 ounces fresh lemon
     juice
  ¾ ounce Rich Simple
     Syrup (P. 16)
  2 blackberries and
     1 lemon wheel
     skewered on a pick,
     for garnish

A variation on the Tom Collins, a summer classic, the Uncle Vanya is best when blackberries are at their seasonal peak.

Fill a cocktail shaker with ice. Add all of the remaining ingredients except the garnish and shake well. Strain into an ice-filled collins glass and garnish with the blackberries and lemon wheel.

◼ apricot and stormy

Ice cubes, plus crushed ice
- 1 ounce vodka
- 1 ounce apricot liqueur
- 1 ounce apricot nectar or juice
- 1 ounce chilled ginger beer
- 1 lime wedge
- 1 dried apricot skewered on a pick, for garnish

Duff particularly likes this fruity drink with spicy Caribbean, Indonesian and Indian foods like jerk chicken, beef rendang (beef cooked in coconut milk) and lamb tikka.

Fill a cocktail shaker with ice cubes. Add the vodka, apricot liqueur and apricot nectar and shake well. Strain into a crushed-ice-filled rocks glass, then top with the ginger beer. Squeeze the lime wedge over the drink and add it to the drink. Garnish with the skewered apricot.

◼ italian berry mule

- 6 raspberries

Ice
- 2 ounces vodka
- ½ ounce fresh lime juice
- ¼ ounce Rich Simple Syrup (P. 16)
- ½ teaspoon aged balsamic vinegar
- 2 ounces chilled ginger beer

Duff updated the Moscow Mule (vodka, lime juice and ginger beer) by adding raspberries and then amplifying the berry flavor with balsamic vinegar.

In a cocktail shaker, muddle the raspberries. Add ice and all of the remaining ingredients except the ginger beer and shake well. Strain the drink into an ice-filled highball glass and stir in the ginger beer.

58

vodka,
aquavit & genever

Y courtesan cocktail

Ice
- 2 ounces Sauvignon Blanc or other crisp white wine
- 1 ounce vodka, preferably Cîroc
- ½ ounce St-Germain elderflower liqueur or elderflower syrup
- ¼ ounce crème de cassis (black-currant liqueur)
- 1 lemon twist, for garnish

Elderflower syrup and crème de cassis— both of which pair exceptionally well with sparkling wine—give this white wine-based cocktail a lovely scent.

Fill a pint glass with ice. Add all of the remaining ingredients except the garnish and stir well. Strain into a chilled martini glass. Pinch the lemon twist over the drink, rub it around the rim of the glass, then drop it into the drink.

Y mango and tarragon martini

- 1 medium mango—peeled, pitted and chopped— plus 1 triangular piece of mango skin for garnish (optional)
- 12 tarragon leaves, plus 2 leaves for garnish

Ice
- 2½ ounces vodka
- ½ ounce fresh lemon juice
- ½ ounce Rich Simple Syrup (P. 16)

Although cocktail snobs might scoff at flavored martinis, Duff feels that this is one of his best creations.

In a cocktail shaker, muddle the mango. Smack the 12 tarragon leaves (p. 24) over the shaker. Add them to the shaker with all of the remaining ingredients except the garnishes; shake well. Strain into a chilled martini glass. Garnish with the mango skin. Smack the remaining tarragon over the drink and add it to the drink.

59

Y incan

One 2-by-1-inch strip of
seeded fresh Asian
red chile

Ice

1 ounce vodka

1 ounce vanilla vodka

1 ounce Cognac

½ ounce Grand Marnier

½ ounce dark crème
de cacao

1 orange twist, flamed
(P. 14), for garnish

*Duff thinks the Incan is an even better
dessert drink "with a tiny cube of
99 percent cacao chocolate on the side."*

In a cocktail shaker, muddle the chile. Add
ice and all of the remaining ingredients
except the garnish and shake well. Double
strain (p. 14) into a chilled martini glass
and garnish with the flamed orange twist.

Y caffè romano martini

Ice

1½ ounces vodka

½ ounce coffee liqueur

2 ounces chilled brewed
espresso

½ ounce elderflower syrup

¼ ounce Rich Simple
Syrup (P. 16)

3 coffee beans and
1 lemon verbena leaf
(optional), smacked
(P. 24), for garnish

*On a trip to Helsinki, Duff drank an
espresso romano (an espresso served
with a piece of lemon zest). When
he returned home, he tinkered with
ingredients behind the bar and
created this drink.*

Fill a cocktail shaker with ice. Add all
of the remaining ingredients except the
garnishes and shake very well. Strain into
a chilled martini glass and garnish with
the coffee beans and lemon verbena leaf.

60

Caffè Romano Martini

*"Coco" martini glass by
William Yeoward.*

Y clubland

Ice
- 2 ounces vodka
- 2 ounces dry white port
- 1 or 2 dashes of Angostura bitters
- 1 lemon twist, for garnish

"This just may be my favorite vodka cocktail," says Duff. It's from the 1937 Café Royal Cocktail Book.

Fill a pint glass with ice. Add the vodka, port and bitters and stir well. Strain into a chilled martini glass. Pinch the lemon twist over the drink, rub it around the rim of the glass and drop it into the drink.

Y northern light

Ice
- 1½ ounces aquavit
- 1½ ounces honey vodka, or 1½ ounces vodka mixed with ½ teaspoon honey
- 4 dashes of orange bitters
- ¾ ounce Cointreau or other triple sec
- 1 orange twist, flamed (P. 14), for garnish

In this twist on the classic Bee's Knees, Duff combines the drink's trademark honey flavor with aquavit's anise and caraway tones.

Fill a pint glass with ice. Add all of the remaining ingredients except the garnish and stir well. Add the flamed orange twist to a chilled martini glass, then strain the drink into the glass.

62

vodka,
aquavit & genever

▮ coexistence collins

Ice
- 2 ounces vodka, preferably Russian
- 2 teaspoons kümmel (caraway liqueur), or 1½ teaspoons aquavit mixed with ½ teaspoon Rich Simple Syrup (P. 16)
- 1 ounce fresh lemon juice
- ½ ounce Rich Simple Syrup (P. 16)
- 1 ounce chilled club soda
- 1 lemon twist, for garnish

The name of this drink refers to the end of the Cold War, which allowed full-flavored Russian vodka to flow freely into the West.

Fill a cocktail shaker with ice. Add all of the remaining ingredients except the club soda and the garnish and shake well. Strain into an ice-filled collins glass and top with the club soda. Pinch the lemon twist over the drink, rub it around the rim of the glass, then drop it into the drink.

⏺ northern monarch

Ice
- 2 ounces aquavit
- 1 ounce fresh lemon juice
- ½ ounce elderflower syrup
- ½ ounce Rich Simple Syrup (P. 16)
- 2 dashes of orange bitters
- 5 mint leaves, smacked (P. 24), plus 1 mint leaf for garnish
- 1 orange twist, for garnish

While unsuccessfully attempting to create "a better mojito," Duff came up with this aquavit-based summer-afternoon drink.

Fill a cocktail shaker with ice. Add all of the remaining ingredients except the garnishes and shake well. Double strain (p. 14) into a chilled martini glass. Pinch the orange twist over the drink, rub it around the rim of the glass, then drop it into the drink. Garnish with the remaining mint leaf.

￼ wormwood candy

Ice

1½ ounces aquavit

1½ ounces chilled fino
sherry

Dash of absinthe

Dash of orange bitters

Sweet Blueberry Foam
(below; optional)

3 blueberries skewered
on a pick, for garnish

*This drink is adapted from one Duff
served at a cocktail-festival dinner in
New Orleans. The dash of absinthe made
it delicious with the dish it accompanied:
crawfish and spinach spiked with
Herbsaint, the anise-flavored liqueur.*

Fill a pint glass with ice. Add the aquavit,
sherry, absinthe and bitters and stir well.
Strain into a chilled martini glass. Spray
the Sweet Blueberry Foam on top and
garnish with the skewered blueberries.

SWEET BLUEBERRY FOAM

In a cream whipper (see Note), combine
2 large egg whites, 2 ounces blueberry
liqueur or syrup, ½ ounce fresh lemon
juice, ½ ounce Rich Simple Syrup (p. 16)
and 2 ounces water. Seal the canister,
shake hard and charge according to
package directions with 1 or 2 nitrous
oxide chargers. Refrigerate for 2 hours.
Makes enough to top 4 to 6 cocktails.

NOTE Cream whippers and nitrous oxide
chargers are available at surlatable.com.

64

Wormwood Candy

"McCleary" martini glass by Juliska;
"Melissa" dish by William Yeoward.

■ the jacob

Ice
2 ounces genever
1 ounce St-Germain
elderflower liqueur
1 lemon twist,
for garnish

*Genever is a Dutch spirit typically
made from a mixture of malted barley,
wheat, corn and rye that's flavored
with juniper and often aged in oak
casks. Duff describes it as being
"close to good whiskey."*

Fill a pint glass with ice. Add the genever
and elderflower liqueur and stir well.
Strain into an ice-filled rocks glass. Pinch
the lemon twist over the drink, rub it
around the rim of the glass, then drop
it into the drink.

■ the wild colonial

2 ounces genever
1 teaspoon single-malt
Scotch
¼ ounce honey mixed
with ¼ ounce water
½ ounce Cinnamon
Syrup (P. 169)
¾ teaspoon *sambal oelek*
or other chile sauce
¼ grapefruit and ½ lime,
cut into chunks
Ice

*This drink was inspired by the Dutch East
India Company, which dominated the
world spice trade in the 1600s and 1700s
and brought ingredients like cinnamon
and Indonesian sambal to the Netherlands.*

In a pint glass, stir the genever with the
Scotch, honey mixture, Cinnamon Syrup
and *sambal*. In a rocks glass, muddle
the grapefruit and lime chunks, then fill
the glass with ice. Pour the cocktail into
the glass and stir well.

vodka,
aquavit & genever

■ vanilla-berry crush

1 lemon, ends discarded,
  cut into wedges
3 large strawberries,
  hulled
Crushed ice
1 ounce genever
1 ounce crème de fraise
  or other good-quality
  strawberry liqueur
1 ounce vanilla liqueur

Duff uses jonge *(or new-style) genever for this drink because it's lighter than the malty* oude *(old-style) genever or the even maltier* korenwijn. *He recommends the Vanilla-Berry Crush for outdoor get-togethers: "It's very much a sunny-summer-afternoon party drink."*

In a rocks glass, muddle the lemon wedges and strawberries. Fill the glass with crushed ice, then add the genever, crème de fraise and vanilla liqueur. Pour the drink into a pint glass and then back into the rocks glass; pour back and forth 3 or 4 more times to mix well. Serve the cocktail in the rocks glass.

gin

LEFT TO RIGHT Delta, P. 75; Gone Native and Kyoto No. 2, P. 74

Details, left to right: Highball glass by Nasonmoretti from Seguso; "Ophelia" highball glass by Lubos Metelák for Moser; tumbler by Lobmeyr.

ANGUS WINCHESTER

It's probably no coincidence that British-born Angus Winchester's specialty is gin, the unofficial spirit of the British navy: Like the famous fleet, Winchester is a world traveler. This may also explain why his drinks (like the yuzu wine–spiked Delta, p. 75) have such a global flavor. Winchester began bartending to earn money to travel, then founded Alconomics, an international bartender-training service, in 2003. An ardent collector of martini pitchers, Winchester drinks only gin martinis (of course) and experiments endlessly with the spirit in a quest for perfection.

"ABSENCE OF ROSE" WALLPAPER BY
VIVIENNE WESTWOOD FOR COLE & SON.

gin

▼ spring feeling

Ice
1½ ounces gin, preferably
     London dry
¾   ounce fresh lime
     juice
¾   ounce green
     Chartreuse
1   cherry blossom,
     for garnish
     (optional)

Winchester has noticed a proliferation of very dry cocktails like the Aviation and numerous martinis on bar menus lately. Spring Feeling—which is extra-dry—is a nod to that trend.

Fill a cocktail shaker with ice. Add the gin, lime juice and Chartreuse and shake well. Strain the drink into a chilled coupe and garnish with the cherry blossom.

▼ north utsire

Ice
1½ ounces gin, preferably
     London dry
½   ounce fresh lime juice
⅓   ounce ginger syrup
2   dashes of rhubarb
     bitters (optional)
1   orange twist, for
     garnish

North Utsire (oot-SEAR-uh) is one of 31 sea areas surrounding the U.K. The areas are recited four times daily in the Shipping Forecast, *a BBC radio broadcast; many listeners love its repetitive, hypnotic quality.*

Fill a cocktail shaker with ice. Add all of the remaining ingredients except the garnish and shake well. Double strain (p. 14) into a chilled coupe and garnish with the orange twist.

mediterranean pink lady

1½ ounces gin, preferably London dry
½ ounce Cointreau or other triple sec
¼ ounce limoncello
¼ ounce Campari
½ ounce fresh lemon juice
1 large egg white
Ice
3 or 4 thin strips of lemon zest, for garnish

Winchester loves limoncello and Campari and wanted to combine them in a classic-style (that is, not overly esoteric or fussy) cocktail. The result is a pretty pink drink that's citrusy and crisp.

In a cocktail shaker, combine all of the ingredients except ice and the garnish and shake well. Add ice and shake again. Strain the drink into a chilled coupe and garnish with the lemon zest.

plosive

6 cardamom pods
2 pinches of freshly ground black pepper
Ice
2 ounces gin, preferably London dry
1 ounce fresh lime juice
½ ounce honey mixed with ½ ounce water
1 lime wheel, for garnish

"With so many distillers using cardamom in their gin, it seemed obvious to make a drink with it," says Winchester. And because gin often has a peppery quality, he added freshly ground pepper as well.

In a cocktail shaker, lightly muddle the cardamom and pepper. Add ice and all of the remaining ingredients except the garnish and shake well. Double strain (p. 14) into a chilled coupe and garnish with the lime wheel.

Mediterranean Pink Lady

"Abysse" coupe by Baccarat.

gone native

Ice

1½ ounces gin, preferably London dry

½ ounce Pimm's No. 1

1 ounce guava juice

1 ounce unfiltered apple juice

½ ounce fresh lemon juice

1 teaspoon Simple Syrup (P. 16)

4 mint leaves, plus 1 mint sprig, smacked (P. 24), for garnish

1 or 2 guava slices, for garnish

London dry gin and Pimm's No. 1 (a gin-based English aperitif) provide the foundation for this cocktail. The guava and other juices give it a tiki-esque feel, says Winchester.

Fill a cocktail shaker with ice. Add all of the remaining ingredients except the mint sprig and guava slices and shake well. Strain the drink into an ice-filled collins or highball glass and garnish with the mint sprig and guava slices.

kyoto no. 2

10 mint leaves, plus 1 mint sprig for garnish

Ice

1½ ounces gin, preferably London dry

¾ ounce fresh lime juice

½ ounce passion fruit nectar or juice

1 ounce chilled tonic water

England's Fever-Tree tonic water (available in U.S. grocery and specialty stores) has a refreshing astringency that makes it Winchester's choice for this tangy, mint-infused drink.

In a cocktail shaker, muddle the mint leaves. Add ice and the gin, lime juice and passion fruit nectar and shake well. Strain into an ice-filled rocks glass, stir in the tonic and garnish with the mint sprig.

74

gin

■ delta

Ice cubes, plus crushed ice
- 1 ounce gin, preferably London dry
- 1 ounce yuzu wine
- ¾ ounce strained strawberry puree
- ¾ ounce Rich Simple Syrup (P. 16)
- ¾ ounce fresh lemon juice
- 3 or 4 kumquat wheels (optional) and 1 mint sprig, for garnish

Yuzu wine is made from the Japanese citrus fruit that tastes like a combination of lemon, lime and grapefruit. Kiuchi brand wine, a good option, is sold online and in specialty wine stores.

Fill a cocktail shaker with ice cubes. Add all of the remaining ingredients except the crushed ice and garnishes and shake well. Double strain (p. 14) the drink into a crushed-ice-filled highball glass and garnish with the kumquat wheels and mint sprig. Serve with a straw.

▼ green grow

Ice
- 1½ ounces Old Tom gin
- 1 ounce dry vermouth
- ½ ounce St-Germain elderflower liqueur
- 2 dashes of celery bitters
- 1 grapefruit twist, for garnish

Winchester favors the lightly sweet Old Tom gin in this pleasantly tart drink.

Fill a pint glass with ice. Add all of the remaining ingredients except the garnish and stir well. Strain into a chilled coupe and garnish with the grapefruit twist.

■ alejandro

Ice
2 ounces gin
¾ ounce Licor 43
   (citrus-and-vanilla-
   flavored liqueur)
1½ ounces heavy cream
Caramelized Angostura
   bitters (see Note) or
   2 dashes of Angostura
   bitters, for garnish

*According to Winchester, "Creamy drinks
have had a rough time in the world of
modern mixology," so he decided to create
one out of sheer "bloody-mindedness"
(British lingo for cantankerousness).*

Fill a cocktail shaker with ice. Add the
gin, Licor 43 and cream and shake well.
Strain the drink into a chilled rocks
glass and garnish with the bitters.

NOTE To caramelize bitters (which
makes the drink more fragrant), add
a small amount to a small, clean spray
bottle (widely available at drugstores).
Spray the bitters over the drink 3 times,
simultaneously flaming the vapor
by holding a lit match over the drink.

76

Alejandro

*"Roland" glass by
Theresienthal.*

⏥ softly softly

2 ounces gin, preferably
London dry
1 ounce dry vermouth
2 teaspoons peach liqueur
2 teaspoons fresh
lemon juice
1 teaspoon orgeat
(almond-flavored syrup)
½ large egg white
Ice
3 dashes of lemon bitters
or 1 lemon twist,
for garnish

This peach-scented cocktail gets its frothy texture from a shaken egg white.

In a cocktail shaker, combine all of the ingredients except ice and the garnish and shake well. Add ice and shake again. Strain the drink into a chilled coupe and garnish with the bitters.

■ english peach smash

¼ peach, plus 1 peach
wedge for garnish
4 or 5 mint leaves, plus
1 mint sprig for garnish
Crushed ice
2 ounces gin
½ ounce Simple Syrup (P. 16)
1 teaspoon crème de
pêche (peach liqueur)
1 lemon wedge, plus
1 lemon wedge for
garnish

"Orchard fruits go so well with gin," says Winchester. In this summery drink, he pairs the spirit with muddled fresh peach.

In a cocktail shaker, muddle the peach quarter with the mint leaves. Add crushed ice and all of the remaining ingredients except the garnishes and shake well. Strain the drink into a crushed-ice-filled rocks glass and garnish with the peach wedge, lemon wedge and mint sprig.

78

gin

♆ chocolate segment

Ice
- 2 ounces gin, preferably London dry
- ¼ ounce Campari
- ¼ ounce Grand Marnier
- ¼ ounce dark crème de cacao
- 1 orange twist, flamed (P. 14), for garnish

The name of this orange-and-chocolate-flavored drink was inspired by a popular candy called Terry's Chocolate Orange, a chocolate sphere that's divided into individual segments and covered in orange foil.

Fill a pint glass with ice. Add all of the remaining ingredients except the garnish and stir well. Strain into a chilled coupe and garnish with the flamed twist.

♆ white rabbit

Ice
- 2 ounces gin, preferably London dry
- ½ ounce anisette liqueur
- 1½ ounces heavy cream
- ½ ounce Simple Syrup (P. 16)
- Small pinch of freshly grated nutmeg, for garnish

Not a fan of anisette liqueur, Winchester challenged himself to make a delicious drink with it. The result is this creamy, spicy cocktail.

Fill a cocktail shaker with ice. Add all of the remaining ingredients except the garnish and shake well. Strain the drink into a chilled coupe and garnish with the nutmeg.

tequila

Red Sangrita, P. 86

Details, left to right: "Stockholm" schnapps glasses by Giarimi from Huset; rocks glass by Aldo Bakker for t.e. from CITE.

JACQUES BEZUIDENHOUT

Although he's originally from a place that isn't known for tequila (South Africa), Jacques Bezuidenhout discovered a passion for it after moving to San Francisco and working with Julio Bermejo to open Tres Agaves in 2005. In just five years he's become one of the world's foremost authorities on the spirit. The director of the bar program at San Francisco's renowned Fifth Floor, Bezuidenhout says tequila is for all seasons, not just summer; he's partial to it mixed with Guinness and port in the warming Black Opal (p. 92).

tequila

■ ginger smash

3 quarter-size slices of peeled fresh ginger
Ice
1½ ounces blanco tequila
1½ ounces sake
1¼ ounces fresh Ruby Red grapefruit juice
¼ ounce Simple Syrup (P. 16)
1 small grapefruit wheel, for garnish

Bezuidenhout is a big fan of tequila with sushi and always thought the spirit would combine well with sake, sushi's more traditional partner.

In a cocktail shaker, muddle the ginger. Add ice and all of the remaining ingredients except the garnish and shake well. Strain into an ice-filled rocks glass and garnish with the grapefruit wheel.

▼ indian summer

3 cardamom pods
Ice
1½ ounces blanco tequila
¾ ounce Pimm's No. 1
1 ounce unsweetened pineapple juice
¼ ounce fresh lime juice
¼ ounce Simple Syrup (P. 16)
1 lime twist, for garnish

"I love the aroma of cardamom," says Bezuidenhout, "and it works well with the spice in tequila."

In a cocktail shaker, lightly muddle the cardamom. Add ice and all of the remaining ingredients except the garnish and shake well. Double strain (p. 14) into a chilled coupe; garnish with the twist.

jalisco sling

Ice
1½ ounces blanco tequila
½ ounce gin
½ ounce cherry Heering
(cherry liqueur)
½ ounce ginger liqueur
¾ ounce fresh lemon juice
1 ounce chilled club soda
1 lemon wheel and
1 brandied cherry
skewered on a pick,
for garnish

Bezuidenhout likes this fruity drink on warm summer evenings with spicy Asian food like Thai green curry.

Fill a cocktail shaker with ice. Add all of the remaining ingredients except the club soda and the garnish and shake well. Strain into an ice-filled highball glass. Stir in the club soda and garnish with the skewered lemon wheel and cherry.

 # harvest crush

Ice
1½ ounces blanco tequila
1½ ounces Alsace Pinot
Gris or other crisp
white wine
½ ounce St-Germain
elderflower liqueur
1¼ ounces white peach
puree, or 1½ ounces
peach nectar or juice
2 peach slices, for garnish

To balance the peppery blanco tequila and spicy Alsace Pinot Gris, Bezuidenhout adds sweet white peach to this drink.

Fill a cocktail shaker with ice. Add all of the remaining ingredients except the garnish and shake well. Strain the drink into an ice-filled highball glass and garnish with the peach slices.

84

Jalisco Sling

*"Ultima Thule" highball glass
by Tapio Wirkkala for Iittala.*

■ red sangrita

MAKES 6 DRINKS

15 ounces tomato juice
7 ounces fresh orange juice
3 ounces fresh grapefruit juice
1¼ ounces fresh lime juice
2 ounces hot sauce
½ jalapeño (with seeds for a spicier drink)
1½ teaspoons freshly ground pepper
1 teaspoon salt
About 9 ounces blanco tequila

In Mexico, sangrita is traditionally served well chilled and accompanied by a good tequila served neat.

In a large container, combine all of the ingredients except the tequila and stir until the salt is dissolved. Let stand for 15 minutes (30 minutes for a spicier drink). Discard the jalapeño and refrigerate the sangrita until chilled, about 2 hours. Stir well and pour into rocks glasses. Serve with shots of tequila alongside.

■ moscato d'agave

2 thin jalapeño slices, seeded
1 ounce white peach puree, or 1¼ ounces peach nectar or juice
¼ ounce fresh lime juice
Ice
1¾ ounces blanco tequila
¾ ounce Muscat
1 lime wheel, for garnish

Bezuidenhout prefers using Quady Winery's Elysium Black Muscat for this spicy drink. He loves its deep, round sweetness, rosy scent and lychee-like flavor with the jalapeño's heat.

In a cocktail shaker, muddle the jalapeño slices with the peach puree and lime juice. Add ice and the tequila and Muscat and shake well. Strain into an ice-filled rocks glass and garnish with the lime wheel.

86

tequila

besito

Ice
1½ ounces reposado tequila
½ ounce Cointreau or
   other triple sec
1 ounce apricot nectar
   or juice
½ ounce fresh lemon juice
¼ ounce agave nectar
   mixed with ¼ ounce
   water
1 ounce chilled
   sparkling wine
1 lemon wedge, for garnish

This sparkling, apricot-accented cocktail is a take on the early-20th-century drink French 75 (gin, Champagne, lemon juice and sugar). Besito *means "little kiss."*

Fill a cocktail shaker with ice. Add all of the remaining ingredients except the sparkling wine and the garnish and shake well. Strain into an ice-filled highball glass, stir in the sparkling wine and garnish with the lemon wedge.

st. rosemary

Leaves from a 1-inch
   rosemary sprig, plus
   1 rosemary sprig for
   garnish
¼ ounce fresh lime juice
Ice
1¾ ounces reposado
   tequila
¾ ounce St-Germain
   elderflower liqueur
1¼ ounces apple juice,
   preferably unfiltered

This cocktail is best with unfiltered apple juice because it tastes more like real apples than the clear kind and retains some of the fruit's natural acidity.

In a cocktail shaker, muddle the rosemary leaves with the lime juice. Add ice and all of the remaining ingredients except the garnish and shake well. Double strain (p. 14) into a chilled coupe and garnish with the rosemary sprig.

87

one hot minute

Ice

1¾ ounces blanco
tequila

½ ounce Lillet blanc

1 ounce apple juice,
preferably unfiltered

1 ounce Fresh Cucumber
Juice (below)

¾ teaspoon agave
nectar mixed with
¾ teaspoon water

1½ teaspoons jalapeño
hot sauce

1 jalapeño and
4 to 6 cucumber
wheels, for garnish

This spicy and fruity concoction was Bezuidenhout's entry in Tabasco's 2008 Hottest Bartender Contest. The drink won first prize.

Fill a cocktail shaker with ice. Add all of the remaining ingredients except the garnishes and shake well. Strain the drink into an ice-filled highball glass and garnish with the jalapeño and cucumber wheels.

FRESH CUCUMBER JUICE

In a mini food processor, puree a 1½-inch piece of peeled cucumber and then fine strain the liquid. Makes about 1 ounce.

NOTE Fresh cucumber juice is also available at health-food-store juice bars.

88

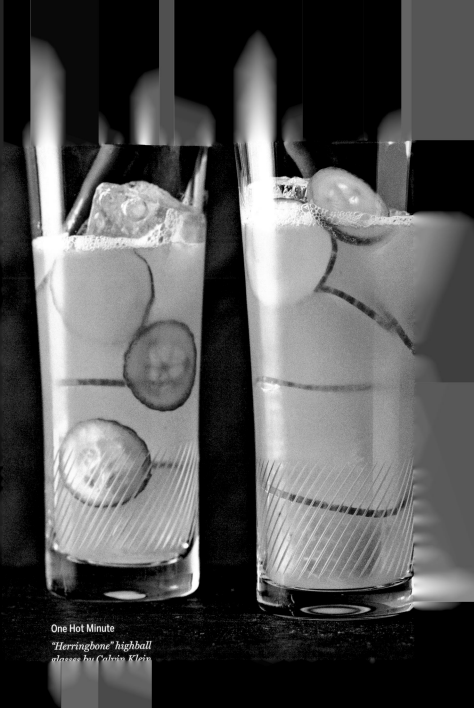

One Hot Minute

*"Herringbone" highball
glasses by Calvin Klein*

la rosa

Ice
1½ ounces blanco tequila
½ ounce crème de mûre
   (blackberry liqueur)
¾ ounce chilled
   strong-brewed
   hibiscus tea
½ ounce fresh lime juice
¾ teaspoon agave nectar
   mixed with ¾ teaspoon
   water
1 thin lime wheel,
   for garnish

Bezuidenhout created this fruity aperitif-style cocktail for the San Francisco restaurant Tres Agaves. Tart hibiscus tea gives the drink its striking rose color.

Fill a cocktail shaker with ice. Add all of the remaining ingredients except the garnish and shake well. Double strain (p. 14) into a chilled coupe and garnish with the lime wheel.

▮ repo cup

Ice
1½ ounces reposado
   tequila
¾ ounce yellow
   Chartreuse
¼ ounce fresh lemon juice
2 ounces chilled bitter
   lemon soda
2 or 3 cucumber wheels,
   for garnish

Bitter lemon soda is a classic English mixer, says Bezuidenhout. He combines it with reposado tequila in this version of the Pimm's Cup, another quintessentially British beverage.

Fill a highball glass with ice. Add the tequila, Chartreuse and lemon juice and stir well. Stir in the lemon soda and garnish with the cucumber wheels.

La Rosa

"Pearl Embroidery"
Champagne glasses by
Giarimi from Huset.

■ black opal

Ice
1½ ounces reposado
    tequila
1½ ounces Guinness
½ ounce tawny port
¼ ounce agave nectar
    mixed with ¼ ounce
    water
Dash of Angostura bitters
1 very small pinch
    of cinnamon mixed
    with 1 pinch of sugar,
    for garnish

Before adding the Guinness to the cocktail shaker, pour some of it into a glass and stir with a bar spoon for about 30 seconds. This releases some of the beer's volatile CO_2, which could cause a mess if the shaker is not sealed well.

Fill a cocktail shaker with ice. Add all of the remaining ingredients except the garnish and shake well. Strain into a chilled rocks glass and garnish with the cinnamon sugar.

♆ agave reviver no. 1

Ice
1¾ ounces reposado
    tequila
1 ounce Calvados
½ ounce green
    Chartreuse
5 dashes of
    Peychaud's bitters
2 dashes of
    Angostura bitters
1 orange twist,
    for garnish

The classic Corpse Reviver No. 1 is a potent combination of brandies and vermouth that's meant to be a hangover remedy. Bezuidenhout created this tequila-based version in the same spirit.

Fill a pint glass with ice. Add all of the remaining ingredients except the garnish and stir well. Strain into a chilled coupe and garnish with the orange twist.

92

tequila

■ en fuego

Ice
1¾ ounces añejo tequila
1 ounce fresh lime juice
¾ ounce agave nectar
¼ ounce single-malt
   Scotch
1 lime wheel, for garnish

En fuego (on fire) refers to the smoky quality of the Laphroaig single-malt whisky that Bezuidenhout uses in this margarita. "I would enjoy the En Fuego after dinner," he says. "Maybe with a cigar."

Fill a cocktail shaker with ice. Add the tequila, lime juice and agave nectar and shake well. Strain into an ice-filled rocks glass, top with the Scotch and garnish with the lime wheel.

� port wine cocktail no. 3

Ice
1¼ ounces mezcal
1¼ ounces port, preferably
   Fonseca Bin No. 27
2 teaspoons Grand
   Marnier
Dash of Angostura bitters
Dash of orange bitters
1 orange twist, for
   garnish

This aromatic after-dinner cocktail is an adaptation of the Port Wine Cocktail No. 2 from Harry Craddock's Savoy Cocktail Book, *first published in 1930.*

Fill a pint glass with ice. Add all of the remaining ingredients except the garnish and stir well. Strain into a chilled coupe and garnish with the orange twist.

maguey sour

Ice
2 ounces mezcal
½ ounce Bénédictine (brandy-based herbal liqueur)
¾ ounce fresh lemon juice
½ ounce orgeat (almond-flavored syrup)
½ large egg white
Pinch of freshly grated nutmeg and 1 orange twist, for garnish

Maguey is another name for agave. Roasting the heart of the plant in an earthen pit (as opposed to steaming or baking it, which is done for tequila) is what gives mezcal its smoky flavor.

Fill a cocktail shaker with ice. Add all of the remaining ingredients except the garnishes and shake well. Strain into an ice-filled rocks glass and garnish with the grated nutmeg and orange twist.

 # cafe pacifico

1½ ounces blanco tequila
½ ounce coffee liqueur
4 ounces hot brewed coffee
4 teaspoons sugar mixed with 1 teaspoon cinnamon
¾ ounce chilled heavy cream

Named after one of Bezuidenhout's favorite tequila bars in London, this Mexican-style spiked coffee makes a great winter after-dinner drink.

In a small heatproof snifter, combine the tequila, coffee liqueur and hot coffee. Stir in 4 teaspoons of the cinnamon sugar and top with the heavy cream. Garnish with a little of the remaining cinnamon sugar.

Maguey Sour

*"Lars" double old-fashioned
glass from Crate & Barrel.*

rum

LEFT TO RIGHT La Florida Rum Daisy, P. 100; Luau Daiquiri, P. 99; Tangaroa, P. 100

Details, left to right: "Stockholm" tumbler by Giarimi from Huset; "Alto"
Champagne saucer by Calvin Klein; flute by Roost from Swallow.

STAR MIXOLOGIST

JEFF BERRY

RUM EVANGELIST

Jeff Berry is one of the world's leading rum experts. He's spent the last 20 years collecting vintage and "lost" tiki recipes—predominantly made with rum—and he's writing his sixth book on exotic drinks, Potions of the Caribbean: Lost Cocktails from America's Playground . . . and the People Behind Them. *Still, exotic cocktails and their origins aren't Berry's only obsession: "Don't tell my cardiologist, but nothing pairs better with rum drinks than pork: pork tenderloin, barbecued spareribs or bacon-wrapped anything."*

"MODERN TRELLIS" WALLPAPER BY F. SCHUMACHER & CO.

rum

♈ luau daiquiri

Ice
- 2 ounces white rum, preferably dry
- ¾ ounce fresh lime juice
- ¾ ounce fresh orange juice
- ½ ounce vanilla syrup
- 1 edible orchid or other unscented white flower, for garnish (optional)

"There are several vanilla syrups on the market," says Berry, "but most of them are geared for coffee drinks or desserts." For his Luau Daiquiri, Berry likes Sonoma Syrup Co.'s version (sonomasyrupstore.com) for its "clean, mellifluous taste."

Fill a cocktail shaker with ice. Add all of the remaining ingredients except the garnish and shake well. Strain into a chilled coupe and garnish with the orchid.

♈ hawaiian room

Ice
- 1 ounce white rum
- ½ ounce apple brandy, preferably bonded
- ½ ounce Cointreau or other triple sec
- ½ ounce unsweetened pineapple juice
- ½ ounce fresh lemon juice

According to Berry, this drink was served in New York City in the 1940s at the Hotel Lexington's Hawaiian Room. It's the only tropical cocktail Berry has encountered that uses applejack (American apple brandy). Berry prefers Laird's Applejack, which the Laird family has been making in New Jersey since 1698.

Fill a cocktail shaker with ice. Add all of the remaining ingredients and shake well. Strain into a chilled coupe.

■ la florida rum daisy

Ice
- 2 ounces white rum
- ½ teaspoon yellow Chartreuse
- ½ teaspoon Simple Syrup (P. 16)

Dash of Angostura bitters
- 1 mint sprig, 1 spiral-cut lemon twist (P. 14) and 1 or 2 cherries, for garnish

The "Rum Daissy" appeared in a 1930s book from the famed bar La Florida in Havana. The original recipe called for Bacardi rum, but Berry recommends Cruzan Aged Light Rum from the Virgin Islands, Flor de Caña Extra Dry from Nicaragua or Mount Gay Special Reserve from Barbados.

Fill a rocks glass with ice. Add the rum, Chartreuse, Simple Syrup and bitters and stir well. Garnish with the mint sprig, lemon twist and cherries.

▮ tangaroa

Ice
- 1 ounce white rum
- 1 ounce amber rum
- ¼ ounce amaretto
- 2 ounces mango puree or nectar
- ½ ounce fresh lime juice
- 1 mango slice skewered on a cinnamon stick, for garnish

"Mango never worked as a drink ingredient for me," says Berry. "It just wasn't interesting." Then an 80-year-old ex-tiki-bartender recommended adding almond extract to help bring out the fruit's flavor. Berry tried using amaretto and it did the trick.

Fill a cocktail shaker with ice. Add all of the remaining ingredients except the garnish and shake well. Strain into a chilled flute and garnish with the skewered mango slice.

rum

■ equinox

Ice
- ¾ ounce white rum
- ¾ ounce amber rum
- ½ ounce Velvet Falernum (clove-spiced liqueur)
- ¾ ounce unsweetened coconut milk
- ½ ounce fresh lime juice
- ¼ ounce honey mixed with ¼ ounce water
- 1 lime wedge and 1 edible orchid (optional), for garnish

Berry thinks the cooling coconut milk and honey in the Equinox make it great with spicy Thai stir-fries or Asian curries.

Fill a cocktail shaker with ice. Add all of the remaining ingredients except the garnishes and shake well. Pour (don't strain) into a chilled rocks glass and garnish with the lime wedge and orchid.

 kon-tini

Ice
- 1½ ounces white rum, preferably Virgin Islands
- ¾ ounce ginger liqueur
- ¾ ounce Velvet Falernum
- ½ ounce dark rum
- ¾ ounce fresh lime juice
- 1 spiral-cut lime twist (P. 14), for garnish

When Domaine de Canton ginger liqueur hit the market in 2007, Berry thought it would mix well with falernum, which is spiced with ginger and clove. It did. For the dark rum, he likes to use Demerara rum because of its "smoky, charred-wood taste."

Fill a cocktail shaker with ice. Add all of the remaining ingredients except the garnish and shake well. Strain into a chilled coupe and garnish with the twist.

colonel beach's plantation punch

3 or 4 ice cubes, plus
      crushed ice
  2 ounces dark rum,
      preferably Jamaican
  1 ounce amber rum
  ½ ounce aged rum,
      preferably Barbados
  ½ ounce Velvet Falernum
      (clove-spiced liqueur)
  2 ounces unsweetened
      pineapple juice
  1 ounce fresh lime juice
Dash of Angostura bitters
  ⅛ teaspoon absinthe,
      preferably Pernod
  2 ounces chilled
      ginger beer
  2 pineapple wedges
      and 2 pineapple leaves
      (optional) skewered
      on a pick, for garnish

According to Berry, this cooler is great for summer parties. Multiply each ingredient by the number of guests you're expecting, mix everything except the ginger beer and garnishes in a punch bowl and chill. Add a large block of ice (or ice cubes) and the ginger beer just before serving.

Put the ice cubes in a highball glass. Fill a cocktail shaker with crushed ice. Add all of the remaining ingredients to the shaker except the ginger beer and garnishes and shake well. Add the ginger beer to the shaker and pour (don't strain) into the highball glass. Garnish with the skewered pineapple wedges and leaves.

Colonel Beach's Plantation Punch

*"Palm" pitcher by Giarimi from
Huset; "Sprigs" highball glass by Karen
Feldman for Artel from TableArt.*

espresso bongo

Ice

- 2 ounces amber rum, preferably Barbados
- ¾ ounce Simple Syrup (P. 16)
- ½ ounce fresh lime juice
- ½ ounce fresh orange juice
- ½ ounce passion fruit nectar or juice
- ½ ounce chilled brewed espresso
- ¼ ounce unsweetened pineapple juice

"I'd always wanted to name a drink after the 1959 British beatnik movie Expresso Bongo," *says Berry. After years of experimenting with syrups, he finally realized that actual coffee and fruit juices delivered the flavor he wanted.*

Fill a cocktail shaker with ice. Add all of the remaining ingredients and shake well. Pour (don't strain) the drink into a large chilled rocks glass.

maracaibo

Ice

- 2 ounces aged rum, preferably Jamaican
- ½ ounce crème de banane
- ¼ ounce St. Elizabeth Allspice Dram (allspice liqueur)
- 3 ounces chilled tamarind nectar
- ½ ounce fresh lemon juice
- 1 lemon wheel, for garnish

Intrigued by the idea of using tamarind in a drink, Berry tinkered with ingredients for over five years before settling on this concoction. It's primarily a hot-weather cocktail, but the allspice dram makes it a good choice for fall and winter, too.

Fill a cocktail shaker with ice. Add all of the remaining ingredients except the garnish and shake well. Pour (don't strain) into a chilled highball glass and garnish with the lemon wheel.

104

rum

■ père labat's punch

Ice
- 2 ounces amber rum, preferably Barbados
- 1 ounce Bajan Spice Syrup (below)
- 1 ounce fresh lime juice
- ¼ ounce chilled club soda

Berry named this winter punch after explorer-priest Père Labat, who chronicled the Caribbean diet in the late 1600s and early 1700s. Labat identified clove, cinnamon and nutmeg as ingredients in a rum punch from Barbados.

Fill a cocktail shaker with ice. Add the rum, Bajan Spice Syrup and lime juice and shake well. Pour (don't strain) the drink into a chilled rocks glass and stir in the club soda.

BAJAN SPICE SYRUP

In a small saucepan, combine 1 tablespoon each of whole cloves, crushed cinnamon stick and cracked or very coarsely grated nutmeg. Add 1 cup water and 1 cup sugar and bring to a boil. Cook over low heat for 15 minutes. Strain the syrup into a heatproof jar and let cool, then cover and refrigerate for up to 1 month. Makes about 10 ounces.

♟ devil's island daiquiri

1 tablespoon sugar
Dash of Fee Brothers
Old Fashion bitters or
Angostura bitters
1 lime wedge
2 ounces spiced rum
1½ tablespoons honey
mixed with 1½
tablespoons softened
unsalted butter
¾ ounce fresh lime juice
½ cup crushed ice

*"This is basically a cold buttered rum,"
says Berry. "You could serve it during
the holidays in lieu of eggnog."*

On a plate, mix the sugar with the bitters.
Moisten the outer rim of a large chilled
coupe with the lime wedge, then coat the
rim with the sugar mixture. In a blender,
combine the rum, honey mixture, lime
juice and crushed ice and blend at high
speed until smooth. Strain through a fine
sieve into the prepared coupe.

♟ coupe d'etat

Ice
1 ounce aged rum
½ ounce cherry Heering
(cherry liqueur)
1 teaspoon Sabra
chocolate-orange
liqueur
½ ounce fresh lime juice
½ ounce fresh orange
juice

*Berry sees this fruity drink as an
aperitif-style cocktail, good anytime
of the year. It's great with Manchego
cheese and, in season, fresh Bing cherries.*

Fill a cocktail shaker with ice. Add all of
the remaining ingredients and shake well,
then strain the drink into a chilled coupe.

106

Devil's Island Daiquiri

"Mitos" coupe by Arik Levy for Květná from Ameico.

whiskey

LEFT TO RIGHT Barm Brack, P. 119; Old Irish Cure, P. 114; Fiestas Patrias, P. 118

Details, left to right: Bowl by Moser; "Mitos" glass by Arik Levy for Květná from Ameico; "Patrician" Champagne cup by Lobmeyr from Neue Galerie; "Kikatsu" zombie glass from Eastern Accent.

SEAN MULDOON

Sean Muldoon is famous in Ireland for making his own cordials as well as the syrups for his exceptional drinks (like the Toasted-Raisin Syrup in his Irish whiskey–based Barm Brack, p. 119). The bar and potations manager at Belfast's Merchant Hotel, he recently finished writing the third volume of The Merchant Hotel Bar Book, *a charming combination of his own inspired creations alongside dozens of classic recipes. Given his druthers, Muldoon always chooses whiskey: "It's the only spirit I drink on its own, and I would opt for a whiskey cocktail over all others."*

"ROMANY DAMASK" WALLPAPER BY ZOFFANY.

whiskey

■ sugar-maple smash

2 lemon wedges
Ice cubes, plus cracked ice
1⅔ ounces Canadian whisky
¼ ounce green Chartreuse
½ ounce unsweetened pineapple juice
¼ ounce pure maple syrup
1 mint sprig, torn into large pieces, plus 1 mint sprig for garnish
1 pineapple chunk, for garnish

A smash is an old-fashioned style of drink that traditionally involves muddling (or "smashing") herbs and sometimes fruit.

In a cocktail shaker, muddle the lemon wedges. Add ice cubes and all of the remaining ingredients except the cracked ice and garnishes and shake well. Strain into a cracked-ice-filled rocks glass. Garnish with the pineapple chunk and mint sprig and serve with a short straw.

■ french canadian

Ice
2 ounces Canadian whisky
½ ounce crème de mûre (blackberry liqueur)
¾ ounce fresh lemon juice
¼ ounce cane syrup or Rich Simple Syrup (P. 16)
4 dashes of absinthe

While this drink possesses a nice "whisky bite," says Muldoon, its floral fruitiness makes it a great introduction to the spirit. If you can't find crème de mûre, substitute crème de cassis (black-currant liqueur), which has a similar berry flavor.

Fill a cocktail shaker with ice. Add all of the remaining ingredients and shake well. Strain into a chilled rocks glass.

♀ lady irish

Ice

⅔ ounce Irish whiskey, preferably Bushmills

⅔ ounce oloroso sherry

½ ounce Red Currant Syrup (below) or grenadine

⅓ ounce fresh lemon juice

1 teaspoon cane syrup or Rich Simple Syrup (P. 16)

1⅔ ounces chilled Champagne

1 small bunch of red currants, for garnish (optional)

Muldoon likes drinking this tart, sherry-spiked Champagne cocktail with shellfish, especially shrimp, lobster or crab.

Fill a cocktail shaker with ice. Add all of the remaining ingredients except the Champagne and the garnish and shake well. Strain the drink into a large chilled coupe and top with the Champagne. Garnish with the red currants.

RED CURRANT SYRUP

In a heatproof bowl, muddle ½ pint of stemmed fresh red currants, cover and let stand at room temperature overnight. Add 1¼ cups superfine sugar and 7 ounces boiling water, stir and let cool completely. Strain the syrup into a jar, cover and refrigerate for up to 1 week. Makes about 12 ounces.

Lady Irish

*"Essence" cocktail glass by
Alfredo Häberli for Iittala.*

♆ old irish cure

Ice

1⅓ ounces Irish whiskey,
preferably Jameson

⅓ ounce dark rum

2½ teaspoons Calvados

⅓ ounce fresh lemon juice

¼ ounce cane syrup or
Rich Simple Syrup (P. 16)

½ teaspoon honey mixed
with ½ teaspoon water

½ teaspoon Fresh Ginger
Juice (below)

Dash of Angostura bitters

1 thin apple slice,
for garnish

*According to the Irish-born Muldoon,
Irish people often drink whiskey
mixed with ginger, honey and lemon
to treat colds. This is a version of
that potion. "With a bit of hot water,"
he says, "it becomes a terrific toddy."*

Fill a cocktail shaker with ice. Add all of
the remaining ingredients except the apple
slice garnish and shake well. Strain the
drink into a chilled coupe and garnish with
the apple slice.

FRESH GINGER JUICE

Press a ¾-inch piece of peeled fresh
ginger in a garlic press, then fine strain
the liquid. Makes about ½ teaspoon.

114

■ highland fling

Ice

1⅓ ounces single-malt Scotch, preferably Highland Park

⅓ ounce dark crème de cacao

¾ ounce fresh lemon juice

⅓ ounce homemade Lapsang Souchong Syrup (below)

1 teaspoon cane syrup or Rich Simple Syrup (P. 16)

2 dashes of Fee Brothers Old Fashion bitters or Angostura bitters

2 ounces chilled ginger ale

1 lemon wedge, for garnish

When Muldoon tried his first cup of Lapsang souchong tea about a year ago, he noticed subtle chocolate notes in addition to the characteristic smokiness. He immediately thought of pairing the tea with a peaty Scotch whisky.

Fill a cocktail shaker with ice. Add all of the remaining ingredients except the ginger ale and the garnish and shake well. Strain into an ice-filled highball glass and stir in the ginger ale. Garnish with the lemon wedge and serve with a long straw.

LAPSANG SOUCHONG SYRUP

In a heatproof bowl, combine ½ cup superfine sugar with 4 ounces hot, strong-brewed Lapsang souchong tea. Let cool, then pour into a jar, cover and refrigerate for up to 1 month. Makes about 6 ounces.

♈ auld alliance

Ice
- 1 ounce single-malt Scotch, preferably Islay
- 1 ounce green Chartreuse
- 1 teaspoon Grand Marnier
- 1 teaspoon Bénédictine (brandy-based herbal liqueur)
- 2 dashes of orange bitters

Pinch of fresh lemon thyme, plus 1 lemon thyme sprig for garnish

Created by Stuart McCluskey of Edinburgh's Bon Vivant bar, the Auld Alliance is Muldoon's perfect after-dinner drink: "herbal, smoky and strong."

Fill a pint glass with ice. Add all of the remaining ingredients except the garnish and stir well. Strain into a chilled coupe and garnish with the lemon thyme sprig.

♈ desert healer

Ice
- 1⅔ ounces blended Scotch
- ⅓ ounce dry vermouth
- 1 teaspoon kirsch
- ¾ ounce fresh clementine juice or orange juice
- ⅔ ounce Simple Syrup (P. 16)
- ½ ounce fresh grapefruit juice
- ⅓ ounce fresh lemon juice
- 1 lemon twist, plus 1 lemon twist for garnish

This drink was inspired by the classic Blood and Sand, but it's drier (thanks to dry vermouth) and more refreshing (it's got three kinds of citrus juice).

Fill a cocktail shaker with ice. Add all of the remaining ingredients except the twists. Pinch 1 lemon twist over the shaker, drop it in and shake well. Strain the drink into a chilled coupe and garnish with the remaining lemon twist.

116

Auld Alliance

*Champagne glass by
Peter Behrens from Ameico.*

fiestas patrias

Ice
- 1 ounce single-malt Scotch, preferably Islay
- ⅔ ounce añejo tequila
- ¾ ounce unsweetened pineapple juice
- ⅔ ounce fresh lime juice
- ½ ounce grenadine, preferably Homemade Grenadine (below)
- 2 dashes of orange flower water
- 1 lime wedge, for garnish

Muldoon modeled the Fiestas Patrias ("patriotic holidays" in Spanish) on the Armillitta Chico, a tequila concoction made with lime, orange flower water and grenadine. He particularly likes the drink with Mexican food.

Fill a cocktail shaker with ice. Add all of the remaining ingredients except the garnish and shake well. Strain into an ice-filled highball glass, garnish with the lime wedge and serve with a long straw.

HOMEMADE GRENADINE

In a medium saucepan, simmer 16 ounces unsweetened pomegranate juice with 1 cup plus 2 tablespoons sugar over moderate heat until thick enough to coat a spoon, about 15 minutes. Let cool, then transfer to a jar, cover and refrigerate for up to 2 weeks. Makes about 16 ounces.

🍷 barm brack

Ice

2 ounces single-malt Irish whiskey

½ teaspoon St. Elizabeth Allspice Dram (rum-based allspice liqueur)

⅔ ounce Toasted-Raisin Syrup (below)

½ ounce heavy cream

1 large egg yolk

Pinch of salt

Pinch of freshly grated nutmeg, for garnish

This creamy, spiced drink honors an Irish Halloween bread called barm brack, which contains currants and raisins. Traditionally, various objects—a coin, a ring, a pea—were baked inside the loaf as a kind of fortune-telling game.

Fill a cocktail shaker with ice. Add all of the remaining ingredients except the garnish and shake well. Strain the drink into a chilled snifter and garnish with the nutmeg.

TOASTED-RAISIN SYRUP

In a medium saucepan, toast 1 cup raisins over moderate heat until fragrant, about 5 minutes. Add 1¼ cups superfine sugar and 7 ounces hot water and simmer for 10 minutes. Let cool completely, then strain into a jar, cover and refrigerate for up to 1 month. Makes about 9 ounces.

■ wheat and barley

Ice
- 1 lemon twist, plus 1 long, thin lemon twist for garnish
- ¾ ounce blended Scotch
- ¾ ounce plum vodka
- 1 teaspoon apricot liqueur
- 1 teaspoon fresh orange juice
- ½ teaspoon fresh lemon juice
- 2 dashes of orange bitters

Muldoon combines plum (vodka) and apricot (liqueur) with citrus to make this pleasantly dry cocktail.

Place the ice in a rocks glass and tuck in the long, thin lemon twist. In a pint glass, combine the Scotch, vodka, apricot liqueur, orange and lemon juices and bitters. Stir well and strain into the prepared rocks glass. Pinch the remaining lemon twist over the drink, rub it around the rim of the glass and discard.

▼ dram of scotch

Cracked ice
- 1 ounce blended Scotch
- ½ ounce sweet vermouth
- ⅓ ounce cherry Heering (cherry liqueur)
- ½ teaspoon St. Elizabeth Allspice Dram
- 1 orange twist, for garnish

This spicy twist on a Rob Roy gets its kick from St. Elizabeth Allspice Dram, a rum-based liqueur flavored with dried pimento (a.k.a. allspice) berries.

Fill a pint glass with cracked ice. Add all of the remaining ingredients except the garnish and stir well. Strain the drink into a chilled coupe and garnish with the orange twist.

Wheat and Barley

*"Drift Ice" double old-
fashioned glass by Moser.*

brandy

LEFT TO RIGHT French Sazerac, **P. 133**; St. Tropez Rhubarb Club, **P. 125**

Details, left to right: Tumblers by Roost from Swallow;
"Rose Stem" porcelain swizzle sticks by Laura Walls Taylor.

ROMÉE DE GORIAINOFF

*Romée de Goriainoff is captivated by
brandy, perhaps because he was born in France,
birthplace of Cognac and Calvados.
With the groundbreaking Experimental Cocktail
Club in Paris and, soon, London, and at
Paris's Curio Parlor (all launched with his childhood
friends Pierre Charles Cros and Olivier Bon),
de Goriainoff is building a cocktail bar empire.
The drink choices include some super-creative
brandy cocktails like his version of the Sazerac,
in which he replaces the usual whiskey
with apple brandy (p. 133).*

brandy

■ ginger curio

Ice cubes, plus crushed ice
1⅔ ounces Cognac
⅔ ounce fresh lime juice
½ ounce Simple Syrup
   (P. 16)
1 quarter-size slice of
   peeled fresh ginger
5 mint leaves, plus 1 mint
   sprig, smacked (P. 24),
   for garnish

"This concoction could be just the thing to ward off a cold," says de Goriainoff, referring to ginger's reputation for boosting immunity. "But the ginger and mint combination also makes it a perfect summer refresher."

Fill a cocktail shaker with ice cubes. Add the Cognac, lime juice, Simple Syrup, ginger and mint leaves and shake briefly. Strain into a crushed-ice-filled rocks glass and garnish with the smacked mint sprig.

st. tropez rhubarb club

1 small rhubarb stalk,
   smashed, plus
   1 or 2 strips of rhubarb
   stalk for garnish
Ice
1⅓ ounces Cognac
⅔ ounce Nardini amaro
   (bittersweet Italian
   liqueur)
2 ounces chilled
   Champagne

The amaro in this unusual sparkling cocktail gives it a pleasing hint of bitterness.

Gently rub the inside of a chilled red wine glass with the smashed rhubarb stalk and discard. Add ice and the Cognac and amaro, then gently stir in the Champagne. Garnish with the strips of rhubarb stalk.

♀ la joie

¼ ounce absinthe

Ice

1⅔ ounces Peach
Cognac (below)

⅔ ounce Simple Syrup
(P. 16)

⅔ ounce fresh lemon
juice

4 dried hibiscus flowers,
plus 1 hibiscus flower
skewered on a pick for
garnish (optional)

*Puree the leftover Cognac-infused
peach for Bellinis, or chop it and add
it to salsa, chutney or vanilla ice
cream. Or simply eat it.*

Rinse a chilled flute with the absinthe
and discard. Fill a cocktail shaker with
ice. Add all of the remaining ingredients
except the garnish and shake well. Strain
into the prepared flute and garnish with
the skewered hibiscus flower.

PEACH COGNAC

Thinly slice one-quarter of a peach. In
a large jar, combine the peach slices with
one 750-ml bottle Cognac and soak for
4 hours or overnight. Discard the peach
slices and refrigerate the Cognac for
up to 1 month. Makes about 24 ounces.

La Joie

*"Silver Band" Champagne tulip by
Dorothy C. Thorpe from Replacements, Ltd.;
"Lulu" decanter by William Yeoward.*

ⵀ experienced

1 lemongrass stalk,
halved crosswise—
bottom half smashed,
top half reserved for
garnish

Ice

1⅔ ounces Cognac

⅔ ounce St-Germain
elderflower liqueur

⅔ ounce fresh lemon juice

2 basil leaves, smacked
(P. 24)

Rubbing the inside of the martini glass with lemongrass gives this drink a fantastic herbal-lemon aroma.

Gently rub the inside of a chilled martini glass with the smashed lemongrass and discard. Fill a cocktail shaker with ice. Add all of the remaining ingredients except the garnish and shake well. Strain into the prepared martini glass and garnish with the lemongrass top.

ⵀ parisian

Cracked ice

1⅓ ounces Cognac

½ ounce Fernet-Branca
(bitter Italian digestif)

½ ounce St-Germain
elderflower liqueur

Dash of Peychaud's bitters

Dash of Angostura bitters

3 brandied cherries,
for garnish

"I love Fernet-Branca!" says de Goriainoff of the potent Italian liqueur. "It adds a distinctive taste to Cognac-based cocktails because it's spicy and bitter, yet dry."

Fill a pint glass with cracked ice. Add all of the remaining ingredients except the garnish and stir well. Strain into a chilled martini glass and garnish with the brandied cherries.

128

brandy

french peruvian

Ice
2/3 ounce Cognac
2/3 ounce pisco
1/3 ounce fresh lime juice
1/3 ounce fresh lemon juice
1/3 ounce Simple Syrup
    (P. 16)
Dash of beaten egg white
    (optional)
Dash of Angostura bitters,
    for garnish

*Here de Goriainoff puts a French spin
on a pisco sour by adding Cognac.*

Fill a cocktail shaker with ice. Add all
of the remaining ingredients except the
garnish and shake well. Strain into a
chilled flute and garnish with the bitters.

ivresse brune

1 teaspoon single-malt
    Scotch, preferably Islay
Ice
1 2/3 ounces Cognac
2/3 ounce Simple Syrup
    (P. 16)
2/3 ounce pure maple
    syrup
1/2 ounce fresh orange
    juice
1/2 ounce fresh lemon juice
Dash of Angostura bitters

*"This is definitely an autumn drink," says
de Goriainoff. "The maple syrup gives it a
caramelized, almost burnt aftertaste," and
rinsing the glass with a peaty Islay Scotch,
such as Laphroaig, adds a smoky note.*

Rinse a chilled coupe with the Scotch.
Fill a cocktail shaker with ice. Add all
of the remaining ingredients and shake
well. Strain into the prepared coupe.

■ lavandou

Ice

1⅔ ounces Cognac

⅔ ounce fresh lemon juice

⅔ ounce Lavender-Honey Syrup (below)

1 fresh lavender sprig, for garnish (optional)

While spending his last summer vacation in the south of France, de Goriainoff was inspired by the fields of lavender all around to create this drink.

In an ice-filled rocks glass, combine all of the ingredients except the garnish. Stir well and garnish with the lavender sprig.

LAVENDER-HONEY SYRUP

Put 2 teaspoons dried lavender on top of an inverted cocktail shaker. Add about ½ ounce Angostura bitters to a small, clean spray bottle (available at drugstores). Spray the bitters over the lavender 6 times, simultaneously flaming the misted bitters with a lit match. Add the lavender to 4 ounces very hot water and let steep for 15 minutes; strain into a small bowl and stir in 4 ounces honey. The syrup can be refrigerated for up to 3 weeks. Makes about 8 ounces.

Lavandou

*"Whisky" double old-fashioned
glass by Oldrich Lipa for Moser.*

ⵣ carina's experience

Ice

⅓ ounce gin, preferably
    Hendrick's

Dash of lavender bitters,
    or pinch of fresh or
    dried lavender

1⅔ ounces Cognac

⅓ ounce Carpano Antica
    Formula (sweet Italian
    vermouth)

Dash of Angostura bitters

De Goriainoff makes this drink with Hendrick's gin, which has the distinction of being produced in Scotland (most gin is English) with cucumbers and rose petals as well as the usual juniper. Lavender bitters (available from cocktailkingdom. com and thebostonshaker.com) add yet another floral note to the drink; the tincture is also excellent in gin-and-tonics.

Fill a pint glass with ice. Add the gin and lavender bitters and stir until slightly diluted. Strain, discarding the liquid and keeping the ice in the pint glass. Add the Cognac, Carpano Antica Formula and Angostura bitters and stir well. Strain the drink into a chilled martini glass.

132

brandy

■ french sazerac

6 sweet apple slices,
plus 1 very thin apple
slice for garnish
¼ ounce absinthe
Ice
1⅔ ounces Calvados
⅓ ounce Simple Syrup
(P. 16)
Dash of Peychaud's bitters

The Sazerac is one of de Goriainoff's favorite drinks. He spikes this version with absinthe-infused apple and uses Calvados in place of the traditional whiskey.

1 On a plate, sprinkle the 6 apple slices with the absinthe. Refrigerate for 2 hours.
2 In a pint glass, lightly muddle the infused apple slices. Add ice and the Calvados, Simple Syrup and bitters and stir well. Double strain (p. 14) into a chilled rocks glass and garnish with the remaining apple slice, pressing it against the inside of the glass.

punches

Indian Summer Cup, P. 143

Details, left to right: Glasses from Crate & Barrel; "Silver Band" punch bowl by Dorothy C. Thorpe from Replacements, Ltd.

WAYNE COLLINS

London-based master bartender Wayne Collins has noticed a worldwide return to "one of Britain's great gifts to the world of drinks: the punch!" Collins, who appears regularly on the BBC show Something for the Weekend, *has been a champion of what he calls "this timeless and oldest form" of cocktail for more than a decade, in part for its communal quality ("It's perfect for social gatherings"). In keeping with the original definition of a punch, however—simply, a mixed drink—he offers a few excellent single-serving punches here, too, like the supercreamy Bourbon Milk Punch (p. 140).*

"BROCATELLO" WALLPAPER BY ZOFFANY.

punches

asia daisy

1 lime, quartered
Ice cubes, plus crushed ice
2 ounces gin
¾ ounce lychee liqueur
¾ ounce Simple Syrup
   (P. 16)
¾ ounce chilled ginger ale
1 fresh or canned lychee
   and 1 mint sprig, for
   garnish

Gin and lychee is one of Collins's favorite flavor combinations. "In a martini, a punch, a sour or even a sweet, cream-based drink, it just seems to work," he says.

In a cocktail shaker, muddle the lime. Add ice cubes and the gin, lychee liqueur and Simple Syrup and shake briefly. Strain into a crushed-ice-filled red wine glass and stir in the ginger ale. Garnish with the lychee and mint sprig.

chinola

Ice
1 lime wedge
1½ ounces white rum
½ ounce crème de pêche
   (peach liqueur)
1 ounce passion fruit
   nectar or juice
½ ounce Simple Syrup
   (P. 16)

While visiting the Dominican Republic, Collins set out to make a daiquiri-like drink using the local Brugal rum and created this sweet-and-sour cocktail. Passion fruit is called chinola *in the D.R.*

Fill a cocktail shaker with ice. Squeeze the lime wedge into the shaker and add it along with all of the remaining ingredients. Shake well, then double strain (p. 14) into a chilled coupe.

sugar hill punch

Ice
- 2 ounces amber rum
- ½ ounce apricot liqueur
- 2 ounces mango nectar or juice
- 1 ounce fresh lime juice
- ½ ounce Simple Syrup (P. 16)
- 4 basil leaves, torn, plus 1 basil sprig for garnish
- 2 dashes of Angostura bitters
- 1 mango slice, for garnish

According to Collins, single-serve punches like this one are a specialty of the Caribbean. "Punch is so versatile, though, that any of them can be made as a single serving or in a large bowl."

Fill a cocktail shaker with ice. Add all of the remaining ingredients except the garnishes and shake well. Strain into an ice-filled highball glass and garnish with the mango slice and basil sprig.

 # chocolate puff

Ice
- 1½ ounces amber rum
- ½ ounce dark crème de cacao
- 1½ ounces heavy cream
- ½ ounce vanilla syrup
- Finely grated zest of ½ small orange
- 1 ounce chilled club soda
- Pinch each of unsweetened cocoa and freshly grated nutmeg, for garnish

Traditional milk punches combine milk with rum and/or brandy, citrus juice, sugar and spices. Adding club soda to this cocktail "gives it a nice puffed-up texture," says Collins. It's terrific as an after-dinner drink.

Fill a cocktail shaker with ice. Add all of the remaining ingredients except the club soda and garnishes; shake well. Strain into an ice-filled highball glass; stir in the soda. Garnish with cocoa and nutmeg.

Sugar Hill Punch

*"Bamboo" tumbler
by Roost.*

gin genie

8 mint leaves
1 ounce gin
1 ounce fresh lemon juice
½ ounce Simple Syrup
   (P. 16)
Crushed ice
1 ounce sloe gin

Collins's eye-catching Gin Genie won Drinks International's 2001 Cocktail Challenge. Its name comes from the David Bowie song "The Jean Genie."

In a highball glass, lightly muddle the mint leaves. Add the gin, lemon juice and Simple Syrup and stir well. Add crushed ice and stir again. Top with more crushed ice and the sloe gin.

 # bourbon milk punch

1½ ounces bourbon
½ ounce dark crème
   de cacao
1 ounce chilled brewed
   espresso
1 scoop vanilla ice cream
Pinch of freshly grated
   nutmeg, for garnish

Typically, Bourbon Milk Punch is made with half-and-half or milk. This frozen version, based on the one served at the New Orleans restaurant Bourbon House, is blended with ice cream—and tastes like a boozy milk shake.

In a blender, combine all of the ingredients except the garnish and blend until smooth. Pour into a small white wine glass and garnish with the nutmeg.

140

Gin Genie

"Lulu" ice bucket and
"Caroline" highball tumbler
by William Yeoward.

bengal lancers' punch

MAKES ABOUT 24 DRINKS

One 1-liter bottle amber rum
One 750-ml bottle Cabernet
    Sauvignon
½ liter curaçao
    or triple sec
16 ounces fresh orange
    juice
16 ounces unsweetened
    pineapple juice
10 ounces fresh lime juice
10 ounces Simple Syrup
    (P. 16)
16 ounces chilled
    sparkling water
Ice, preferably 1 large block
1 sliced orange, 1 sliced
    lime and 1 sliced
    pineapple, for garnish
One 750-ml bottle chilled
    Champagne

"I love old-school colonial punch drinks like this one," says Collins. *"They really capture the eccentricity and decadence of the old British Empire."* Bengal Lancers' Punch *was adapted from a recipe in Charles H. Baker Jr.'s 1939* Gentleman's Companion, *which credits the drink to a "Captain Ferguson, late of His Majesty's Cavalry in upper India."*

In a punch bowl, combine the rum, wine, curaçao, orange juice, pineapple juice, lime juice and Simple Syrup. Refrigerate until chilled, about 4 hours. Stir in the sparkling water, then carefully add the ice and garnish with the orange, lime and pineapple slices. Top with the Champagne.

142

punches

 ## indian summer cup

MAKES ABOUT 24 DRINKS

One 1-liter bottle gin,
    preferably London dry
One 1-liter bottle Carpano
    Antica Formula (sweet
    Italian vermouth)
  8 ounces St-Germain
    elderflower liqueur
  8 ounces crème de pêche
    (peach liqueur)
24 ounces Lemon Syrup
    (below)
16 ounces unfiltered
    apple juice
32 ounces chilled tonic
    water
16 ounces chilled
    sparkling water
Ice
  1 sliced green apple,
    2 sliced peaches,
    6 long, thin cucumber
    slices and ¼ cup torn
    mint leaves (optional),
    for garnish

Collins prefers using premium, naturally sweetened tonic water (sometimes called Indian tonic water) in this punch. Q Tonic, made with agave nectar, and Fever-Tree, sweetened with cane sugar, are both excellent brands. (They're available at amazon.com.)

In a punch bowl, combine the gin, vermouth, elderflower and peach liqueurs, Lemon Syrup and apple juice. Refrigerate until chilled, about 4 hours. Stir in the tonic water and sparkling water. Add ice and garnish with the apple, peaches, cucumber and mint leaves.

LEMON SYRUP

In a pitcher, combine the finely grated zest of 5 lemons with 16 ounces fresh lemon juice and 8 ounces Simple Syrup (p. 16). Refrigerate for 1 hour, stirring occasionally. Strain the syrup into a large container, cover and refrigerate for up to 2 weeks. Makes about 24 ounces.

garrick gin punch

MAKES ABOUT 24 DRINKS

One 1-liter bottle chilled
    genever
One-half 750-ml bottle
    maraschino liqueur
48 ounces Lemon
    Syrup (P. 143)
16 ounces Simple Syrup
    (P. 16)
64 ounces chilled
    sparkling water
Ice, preferably 1 large block
  2 small sliced oranges,
    for garnish

This is an adaptation of a 19th-century recipe from London's Garrick Club, whose members must be voted in. According to the original screening committee, "it would be better that ten unobjectionable men should be excluded than one terrible bore should be admitted."

In a punch bowl, combine the genever with the maraschino liqueur and both syrups. Refrigerate until chilled, about 4 hours. Stir in the sparkling water, then add the ice and garnish with the oranges.

 # italian spritz punch

MAKES ABOUT 20 DRINKS

16 ounces Galliano (Italian
    herbal liqueur)
One 750-ml bottle Aperol
    (bitter orange Italian
    aperitif)
Three 750-ml bottles chilled
    Prosecco
Ice, preferably 1 large block
  2 sliced oranges, 2 sliced
    lemons and ½ pint
    raspberries, for garnish

Agostino Perrone, head mixologist at London's luxurious Connaught Bar, created this simple sparkling punch. "It would be a great aperitif for a large dinner party," says Collins; he recommends serving it in teacups.

In a punch bowl, combine the Galliano and Aperol and refrigerate until chilled, about 4 hours. Gently stir in the Prosecco. Add the ice and garnish with the oranges, lemons and raspberries.

144

Italian Spritz Punch

*Punch bowl and glasses
by Nasonmoretti.*

paradise punch

MAKES ABOUT 20 DRINKS

One 1-liter bottle amber rum

½ liter dark rum

8 ounces apricot liqueur

26 ounces Lime Syrup (below)

16 ounces unsweetened pineapple juice

16 ounces passion fruit nectar or juice

16 ounces chilled sparkling water

Ice, preferably 1 large block

3 sliced oranges, 1 cubed pineapple, 2 cubed mangoes, 1 cubed small watermelon (optional) and ¼ cup torn mint leaves, for garnish

According to Wayne Curtis's 2006 book And a Bottle of Rum, *the English made punch in India as early as 1673. From there, sailors took the drink "along trade routes, to Europe and on to the New World." On the way, "an astonishing number of variations surfaced."*

In a punch bowl, combine the amber and dark rums, apricot liqueur, Lime Syrup, pineapple juice and passion fruit juice and refrigerate until chilled, about 4 hours. Stir in the sparkling water. Add the ice and garnish with the oranges, pineapple, mangoes, watermelon and mint.

LIME SYRUP

In a pitcher, combine the finely grated zest of 5 limes, 16 ounces fresh lime juice and 12 ounces Simple Syrup (p. 16) and mix well. Refrigerate for 1 hour, stirring occasionally. Strain into a large container, cover and refrigerate for up to 2 weeks. Makes about 28 ounces.

punches

 ## imperial brandy punch

MAKES ABOUT 20 DRINKS

One 1-liter bottle Cognac
- ½ **liter amber rum**
- 5 **ounces curaçao or triple sec**
- 10 **ounces fresh lemon juice**
- 6 **ounces Raspberry Syrup (below)**

Two 750-ml bottles chilled Champagne

Ice, preferably 1 large block
- 5 **sliced oranges and 1 cubed pineapple, for garnish**

This sparkling punch appeared in the 1882 edition of Harry Johnson's New and Improved Bartenders' Manual.

In a punch bowl, combine the Cognac, rum, curaçao, lemon juice and Raspberry Syrup and refrigerate until chilled, about 4 hours. Gently stir in the Champagne. Add the ice and garnish with the orange slices and pineapple cubes.

RASPBERRY SYRUP

In a saucepan, combine one 12-ounce jar raspberry jam with 1 cup water. Cook over moderate heat, stirring, until the jam is melted, about 5 minutes. Strain into a heatproof jar and let cool completely. Cover and refrigerate for up to 1 month. Makes about 16 ounces.

mixologist
all-stars

Cholo Fresco, P. 152

*Details, left to right: "Bark" cocktail shaker
by Roost; "Patrician" Champagne cup by
Josef Hoffman for Lobmeyr from Neue Galerie.*

'10

EDITOR'S PICKS

BY JIM MEEHAN

Jim Meehan just might be the world's best cocktail scout. Besides choosing top mixologists to produce the spirits chapters in this book, he also compiled this roundup of drinks from sensational bartenders around the world (Slovakia! Stockholm! Los Angeles!). The deputy editor of FOOD & WINE Cocktails *since 2006, Meehan doesn't just know all the top mixologists, he's one himself: He was named American Bartender of the Year at the 2009 Tales of the Cocktail Spirit Awards for his work at PDT in Manhattan.*

"CHELSEA STRIPE" WALLPAPER BY COLE & SON.

all-stars

valencia

Marian Beke • Montgomery Place, London

Ice
- ¼ ounce apricot eau-de-vie mixed with 1½ teaspoons sugar, or ½ ounce apricot brandy
- 2 dashes of orange bitters

Juice of ½ large orange
- 3 ounces chilled Champagne

According to Beke, this mimosa-like cocktail is said to have been the winning drink in the first-ever official bartender competition, in Vienna, around 1910.

Fill a cocktail shaker with ice. Add all of the remaining ingredients except the Champagne and shake well. Strain into a chilled flute and top with the Champagne.

thamyris

Chris Hannah • Arnaud's French 75 Bar, New Orleans

Ice
- 2 ounces gin
- ½ ounce Cynar (bitter artichoke liqueur)
- ¼ ounce ginger liqueur
- ¼ ounce St-Germain elderflower liqueur
- 1 orange twist, for garnish

Hannah named this pleasantly bitter stirred-gin cocktail after a poet in Greek mythology who boasted that he could sing better than the Muses, challenged them to a contest and lost.

Fill a pint glass with ice. Add all of the remaining ingredients except the garnish and stir well. Strain into a chilled coupe and garnish with the orange twist.

cholo fresco

Hans Hilburg • El Pisquerito, Cuzco, Peru

10 mint leaves, plus 1 mint
   sprig for garnish
2 teaspoons sugar
½ ounce fresh lime juice
Ice
2 ounces pisco
½ ounce melon liqueur
1 ounce Fresh Cucumber
   Juice (P. 88)
1 cucumber blossom, for
   garnish (optional)

At this pisco-themed bar, Hilburg uses local slang to name his cocktails. Cholo fresco *means "somebody who is fresh in every sense," he says. "Light, saucy, naughty, audacious . . . And what's fresher than cucumber, melon, mint and lime?"*

In a pint glass, muddle the mint leaves with the sugar and lime juice. Strain into an ice-filled cocktail shaker. Add the pisco, liqueur and cucumber juice; shake well. Strain into a chilled coupe. Garnish with the cucumber blossom and mint sprig.

her majesty's pearl

Misty Kalkofen • Drink, Boston

Ice
1½ ounces white rum,
   preferably rhum
   agricole
½ ounce Cognac
½ ounce St-Germain
   elderflower liqueur
½ ounce fresh lemon juice
¼ ounce Simple
   Syrup (P. 16)
7 drops of rose water

There is no cocktail list at Drink. Instead, the bartenders mix classic and bespoke cocktails according to their guests' requests. Kalkofen invented this drink for Randy Wong, a regular who requested "something with a floral note."

Fill a pint glass with ice. Add all of the remaining ingredients and stir well. Strain into a chilled coupe.

152

all-stars

genever blush

Nick Kobbernagel • Ruby, Copenhagen

Ice
- ⅔ ounce genever
- ⅔ ounce Lillet blanc
- ⅔ ounce Campari
- ½ passion fruit, or ½ ounce passion fruit nectar or juice
- ⅓ ounce gomme syrup (simple syrup with gum arabic) or Simple Syrup (P. 16)
- 6 to 8 passion fruit seeds, for garnish (optional)

Genever, a distilled, grain-based spirit that originated in Holland, gives this pretty pink aperitif a light malty flavor. Gomme syrup, sometimes known as gum syrup, gives the drink a weightier texture; it's available at smallhandfoods.com.

Fill a cocktail shaker with ice. Add all of the remaining ingredients except the garnish and shake well. Double strain (p. 14) into a chilled coupe and garnish with the passion fruit seeds.

klara friis

Soren Krogh • Le Lion, Hamburg

Ice
- 2½ ounces oloroso sherry
- ¾ ounce Poire Williams
- ¾ ounce aquavit
- Dash of grapefruit bitters or orange bitters

The Poire Williams (pear brandy) in this drink reminds Danish-born Krogh of a variety of pear (Clara Frijs) that his mother got every autumn from a local farm when he was a child. "It's not really fall until I can get my hands on some of these pears," he says.

Fill a pint glass with ice. Add all of the remaining ingredients and stir well. Strain into a chilled coupe.

sunburst

H. Joseph Ehrmann • Elixir, San Francisco

½ kiwi, peeled and
quartered, plus 1 or 2
kiwi slices for garnish

Ice

2 ounces vodka

½ ounce Aperol
(bitter orange Italian
aperitif)

1 ounce Tangerine
Syrup (below)

1 ounce chilled club soda

1 tangerine wheel,
for garnish

Ehrmann particularly likes what the kiwi ("an underutilized fruit") does for this cooler: "It contributes both sweet and sour, like citrus, and gives it a great texture."

In a cocktail shaker, muddle the kiwi. Add ice and the vodka, Aperol and Tangerine Syrup and shake well. Strain into an ice-filled highball glass, top with the club soda and garnish with the kiwi slices and tangerine wheel.

TANGERINE SYRUP

In a small saucepan, combine 8 ounces fresh tangerine juice with 1 cup sugar. Bring to a boil over moderately high heat, stirring to dissolve the sugar, about 3 minutes. Let cool completely, then transfer to a jar, cover and refrigerate for up to 1 week. Makes about 12 ounces.

154

Sunburst

"Library Stripe" tumblers by Kate Spade for Lenox.

celery nori

Don Lee • Momofuku Ssäm Bar, Manhattan

MAKES 8 DRINKS

1 celery rib, finely
  chopped
7 ounces Simple
  Syrup (P. 16)
Ice
16 ounces Nori Apple
  Brandy (below)
16 dashes of celery
  bitters
8 lemon twists,
  for garnish

This savory old-fashioned was inspired by a dish on Ssäm Bar's menu that combined uni (sea urchin) with a celery sauce and a seaweed garnish. Lee thinks the drink pairs especially well with dishes from a raw bar like oysters.

1 In a small bowl, muddle the celery with the Simple Syrup. Let the celery syrup stand for 30 minutes, then strain.
2 Fill 8 rocks glasses with ice. Divide the Nori Apple Brandy, celery syrup and bitters among the glasses and stir well. Garnish each drink with a lemon twist.

NORI APPLE BRANDY

In a large jar or bowl, cover 6$\frac{1}{3}$ sheets of nori with one 750-ml bottle bonded apple brandy. Let infuse for 90 seconds (really) and strain into a container. Cover and keep at room temperature for up to 1 month. Makes about 24 ounces.

156

all-stars

masataka swizzle

Stanislav Vadrna • Paparazzi, Bratislava, Slovakia

Crushed ice
1½ ounces Japanese or
     Scotch blended malt
     whisky
 ½ ounce nut liqueur
 ½ ounce fresh lemon juice
 ½ teaspoon Simple
     Syrup (P. 16)
  2 dashes of orange bitters
  3 dashes of Peychaud's
     bitters, plus 2 dashes
     for garnish
  1 mint sprig, for garnish

Named for Japanese Nikka whisky founder Masataka Taketsuru, this drink was Vadrna's contribution to the Bartenders' Travelling Book. *The tome is going around the world via FedEx to mixologists so that each can record (in longhand) cocktail lore.*

Half fill a rocks glass with crushed ice. Add all of the remaining ingredients except the garnishes. Set a swizzle stick or bar spoon in the glass; spin between your hands to mix. Add more ice and swizzle again. Garnish with the bitters and mint.

el catador

Charles Vexenat • HIX, London

  1 lemon twist, plus
     1 lemon twist for
     garnish
Ice
3 or 4 dashes of Bittermens
     Xocolatl Mole Bitters
     or Angostura bitters
  1 ounce Galliano
     (Italian herbal liqueur)
  1 ounce oloroso sherry,
     preferably Matusalem
  1 ounce añejo tequila

Vexenat uses Tequila Ocho's añejo in this digestif-style cocktail. The earthy tequila is delicious with the nutty oloroso sherry.

Pinch 1 lemon twist over a chilled coupe and discard. Fill a pint glass with ice. Add all of the remaining ingredients except the garnish and stir well. Strain into the prepared coupe and garnish with the remaining lemon twist.

commodore 64

Jason Chan • Seamstress, Melbourne

Ice
1⅓ ounces bourbon
⅔ ounce white crème de cacao
⅔ ounce fresh lemon juice
⅔ ounce fresh orange juice
½ ounce grenadine
Dash of Fee Brothers Old Fashion bitters or Angostura bitters
1 orange wedge, for garnish

This predinner drink is Chan's orange-infused variation on the Commodore No. 2 (bourbon, crème de cacao, lemon juice and grenadine) from the 1935 Old Waldorf-Astoria Bar Book.

Fill a cocktail shaker with ice. Add all of the remaining ingredients except the garnish and shake well. Strain into an ice-filled rocks glass and garnish with the orange wedge.

honey and spice

John Coltharp • Seven Grand, Los Angeles

Ice
2 ounces bourbon
¼ ounce St. Elizabeth Allspice Dram (rum-based allspice liqueur)
¾ ounce fresh lemon juice
1 tablespoon honey mixed with 1 teaspoon water
Dash of Angostura bitters

"Orange flower honey really complements the allspice dram and the bitters," says whiskey expert Coltharp. He particularly likes the Honey and Spice around the December holidays: "It's a cold glass of Kentucky Christmas."

Fill a cocktail shaker with ice. Add all of the remaining ingredients and shake well. Strain into an ice-filled rocks glass.

158

Commodore 64

"Vesta" double old-fashioned tumbler by William Yeoward.

tiger

Linden Pride • Spice Temple, Sydney

2 ounces blended Scotch
½ ounce yellow Chartreuse
¼ ounce orgeat (almond-flavored syrup)
1 large egg white
Ice
Dash of Angostura bitters
Dash of Peychaud's bitters

The frothy, almond-accented Tiger is meant to cool the heat from the spices in chef Neil Perry's regional Chinese cooking.

In a cocktail shaker, combine the Scotch, Chartreuse, orgeat and egg white and shake well. Add ice and shake again. Strain into a chilled rocks glass. Dash the Angostura and Peychaud's bitters across the drink (to mimic tiger stripes).

coffee brown

Jimmy Dymott • f/l Cocktailbar, Stockholm

Ice
1⅔ ounces bourbon
⅔ ounce coffee liqueur
⅔ ounce port, preferably late bottled vintage
4 dashes of orange bitters
1 orange twist, for garnish

The supercool f/l is a bakery by day. At night, Dymott serves inspired creations like this after-dinner drink at the members-only bar.

Fill a pint glass with ice. Add all of the remaining ingredients except the garnish and stir well. Strain into a chilled coupe and garnish with the orange twist.

160

punch royal

David Wondrich • Brooklyn, New York

MAKES ABOUT 24 DRINKS

One 1-liter bottle Cognac
Large strips of zest from
    2 lemons
  1 **pound *panela***
    (Latin American
    solid sugar) or
    light brown sugar
  1 **cinnamon stick**
  1 **teaspoon finely grated**
    fresh ginger
  8 **ounces fresh lemon**
    juice
One-half 750-ml bottle
    chilled dry German
    Riesling
Ice, preferably 1 large block
Freshly grated nutmeg,
    for garnish

"Punch Royal dates back to the end of the 17th century," says cocktail historian David Wondrich. "It was drunk by courtiers, pirates and everyone in between." Wondrich's upcoming book, Punch, or the Delights and Dangers of the Flowing Bowl, *is due out in late 2010 from Perigee Books.*

---

1 In a large container, combine the Cognac and lemon zest strips. Let the mixture stand at room temperature for 6 to 8 hours. Discard the lemon zest. 2 In a large saucepan, combine the sugar, cinnamon stick and ginger with 16 ounces of water. Cook over low heat, stirring, until the sugar dissolves, about 3 minutes. Strain the brown sugar syrup and let cool. 3 In a large punch bowl, combine the infused Cognac, lemon juice and three-quarters of the brown sugar syrup; refrigerate until chilled, about 2 hours. Stir in the Riesling and 32 ounces of chilled water; add more brown sugar syrup to taste. Add the ice and garnish with the freshly grated nutmeg.

mocktails

LEFT TO RIGHT Tropical Delight,
P. 170; Raspberry Fizz, P. 165

*Details, left to right: "Golden
Band" glass by Dorothy C.
Thorpe from Replacements, Ltd.;
"Pebbles" highball glass by Moser.*

SEBASTIAN REABURN

"Cocktails are luxurious, decadent and delicious first. Then they are alcoholic," says Sebastian Reaburn, the author of Complete Cocktails: Stir, Shake & Make. *Reaburn serves outstanding cocktails and mocktails at his bar, 1806, in Melbourne, Australia. He attributes his passion for creative flavor combinations—like the turmeric, cumin and sweet paprika in the Pomme Pomme (p. 172)—to the bland beverages of his childhood. "I think the most interesting drink I had was a vanilla milk shake."*

"CORINTHIAN ACANTHUS" WALLPAPER BY ANYA LARKIN FROM HINSON & COMPANY.

mocktails

 ## raspberry fizz

8 raspberries, plus
   3 raspberries skewered
   on a pick for garnish
Ice
1 ounce fresh lemon juice
1 teaspoon rose water
¾ ounce Simple Syrup
   (P. 16)
2 ounces chilled club
   soda
1 lemon wheel,
   for garnish

"For a while, I was addicted to raspberry sorbet," says Reaburn. "This mocktail is the liquid version of it."

In a cocktail shaker, muddle the 8 raspberries. Add ice and the lemon juice, rose water and Simple Syrup and shake well. Strain into an ice-filled highball glass. Stir in the club soda and garnish with the skewered raspberries and the lemon wheel.

 ## strawberry smash

6 strawberries, plus
   1 strawberry, halved,
   for garnish
6 to 8 mint leaves, plus
   1 mint sprig for garnish
Ice
2 ounces melon puree
   or juice
½ ounce Simple Syrup
   (P. 16)
2 ounces chilled
   club soda

To make a thicker, fruitier version of this summer drink, don't strain it (discarding the muddled mint leaves is optional).

In a cocktail shaker, muddle the whole strawberries and mint leaves. Add ice and the melon puree and Simple Syrup and shake well. Strain into an ice-filled highball glass and stir in the club soda. Garnish with the halved strawberry and mint sprig.

hot fizz

One 1-inch piece of hot chile,
  seeded, plus 1 chile for
  garnish
Ice
  2 ounces unfiltered
    apple juice
  1 ounce fresh lime juice
  ½ ounce Simple Syrup
    (P. 16)
  2 ounces chilled club
    soda
  1 lime wedge, for garnish
    (optional)

"Ask most bartenders about the molecular difference between the acid in citrus and the acid in apples, and they're lost," says Reaburn. In this fizz, he pairs tart apple juice with hot chile, which adds great heat and a zingy, slightly sweet pepper taste.

In a cocktail shaker, gently muddle the piece of chile. Add ice and the apple juice, lime juice and Simple Syrup and shake well. Strain into an ice-filled highball glass. Stir in the club soda and garnish with the chile and lime wedge.

 # lime cubes

  1 ounce fresh lime juice
  1 ounce cold water
  ½ ounce Simple Syrup
    (P. 16)
  1 kaffir lime leaf
    (optional)
  3 cardamom pods
One 2-inch strip of
    lime zest
Ice
  2 ounces chilled
    ginger beer

Reaburn serves this cardamom-accented drink two ways, depending on the weather: on hot days, mixed with ginger beer—as directed in this recipe; on cool ones, strained into a rocks glass over a single large ice cube. The second way makes the flavors more intense.

In a cocktail shaker, combine all of the ingredients except ice and the ginger beer and muddle. Strain into an ice-filled highball glass and stir in the ginger beer.

 166

Hot Fizz

"Golden Leaf Aliseo"
glass by Nasonmoretti;
brass cocktail pick from
Haus Interior.

green refresher

2 cucumber slices
Ice
3 ounces chilled brewed
green tea, preferably
sencha
1 ounce unfiltered
apple juice
¾ ounce Simple Syrup
(P. 16)
½ ounce fresh lime juice
Thin strips of lime zest,
for garnish

Use a zester to cut the garnish over the glass. The peel's essential oils drop into the drink and give it a terrific limy scent.

In a highball glass, muddle the cucumber slices, then half fill the glass with ice. Add all of the remaining ingredients except the garnish and stir well. Add more ice and stir again. Garnish with the lime zest.

tennis reviver

Ice
4 ounces chilled brewed
chamomile tea
1 ounce fresh lemon juice
½ ounce Simple Syrup
(P. 16)
½ ounce elderflower
syrup
1 chamomile flower,
for garnish (optional)

For Reaburn, who got serious about bartending in London, chamomile tea and tennis on a hot summer day are forever linked. This icy chamomile drink "refreshes you while relaxing your muscles; it's the perfect post-exercise beverage," he says.

Half fill a highball glass with ice. Add all of the remaining ingredients except the garnish and stir well. Add more ice and garnish with the chamomile flower.

mocktails

▮ cherry red

6 cherries, pitted, plus
   1 cherry for garnish
Ice
2 ounces cranberry
   juice
1 ounce fresh lemon juice
½ ounce Cinnamon Syrup
   (below)
2 ounces chilled
   club soda

Reaburn uses black cherries when he makes the Cherry Red, which was inspired, he says, by "classic American flavors like Big Red chewing gum and cherry Coke." Add any leftover Cinnamon Syrup to hot toddies, hot chocolates, chai lattes or coffee, or pour it over vanilla ice cream. You can also substitute it for simple syrup in hot or cold holiday drinks.

In a cocktail shaker, muddle the pitted cherries. Add ice and the cranberry juice, lemon juice and Cinnamon Syrup and shake well. Pour into an ice-filled highball glass, stir in the club soda and garnish with the remaining cherry.

CINNAMON SYRUP

In a small saucepan, bring 1 cup water to a boil with 1 cup sugar and 6 medium cinnamon sticks broken into pieces. Simmer over moderate heat for 3 minutes, stirring to dissolve the sugar. Let cool, then cover and let stand for 4 hours. Strain the syrup into a jar, cover and refrigerate for up to 1 month. Makes about 12 ounces.

rocking orange

Ice
- 2 ounces fresh orange juice
- 2 ounces fresh mandarin orange juice or orange juice
- ½ ounce fresh lemon juice
- ½ ounce orange syrup
- 2 ounces chilled club soda
- Thin strips of orange zest and 1 orange twist, for garnish

This terrific brunch mocktail combines multiple forms of citrus fruit: orange, lemon and mandarin orange juices, plus orange syrup and orange peel.

Fill a cocktail shaker with ice. Add all of the remaining ingredients except the club soda and garnishes and shake well. Strain into an ice-filled highball glass, then stir in the club soda. Garnish with the orange zest strips and the twist.

Y tropical delight

Ice
- 2 ounces unsweetened pineapple juice
- 1 ounce passion fruit nectar or juice
- 1 ounce unfiltered apple juice
- ¾ ounce fresh lime juice
- ½ ounce Simple Syrup (P. 16)
- ½ passion fruit, for garnish (optional)

"There was an ice cream I used to eat when I was young that was flavored with passion fruit and pineapple," says Reaburn. "The taste of the Tropical Delight is very similar, and brings back some great memories."

Fill a cocktail shaker with ice. Add all of the remaining ingredients except the garnish and shake well. Strain into a chilled martini glass and float the passion fruit half on top.

170

Rocking Orange

*"Ottagonale"
highball glasses
by Carlo Moretti
from TableArt.*

■ pomme pomme

Ice
- 2 ounces unfiltered apple juice
- 2 ounces pomegranate juice
- ½ ounce Simple Syrup (P. 16; optional)
- ¼ ounce pomegranate molasses
- 3 cumin seeds
- ½ teaspoon sweet paprika
- ¼ teaspoon ground turmeric
- 3 apple slices dusted with sweet paprika and salt, for garnish

Some of Reaburn's favorite bar ingredients are kitchen spices that are rarely seen in drinks, such as the cumin, paprika and turmeric in the Pomme Pomme. Dust any leftover apple with more paprika and salt for a fantastic bar snack.

Fill a cocktail shaker with ice. Add all of the remaining ingredients except the garnish and shake well. Strain the drink into an ice-filled rocks glass. Garnish with the spiced apple slices.

mocktails

 ## earl of the caribbean

½ white peach, peeled, plus
   1 peach slice for garnish
1 ounce cream of coconut
Ice cubes, plus crushed ice
1 ounce unsweetened
   pineapple juice
⅓ ounce Simple Syrup
   (P. 16)
1 teaspoon unsalted butter
4 sage leaves, plus 1 sage
   leaf for garnish
3 ounces chilled brewed
   Earl Grey tea

This creamy, peach-flavored mocktail was inspired by the piña colada. Shaking the drink with a chunk of butter makes it extra-rich.

In a cocktail shaker, muddle the peach half with the cream of coconut. Add ice cubes and the pineapple juice, Simple Syrup, butter and 4 sage leaves and shake well. Double strain (p. 14) into a crushed-ice-filled pilsner glass. Stir in the tea and garnish with the peach slice and sage leaf.

coffee cooler

Ice
5 cardamom pods
3 ounces chilled
   brewed coffee
1 ounce fresh
   orange juice
½ ounce Simple Syrup
   (P. 16)
1 sage sprig, plus 1 sage
   leaf for garnish
1 ounce chilled club soda
1 orange twist,
   for garnish

"Coffee has a much more complex flavor than most people realize," says Reaburn. He brings out its nuances here by adding sage and orange peel.

Fill a cocktail shaker with ice. Add all of the remaining ingredients except the club soda and garnishes and shake well. Double strain (p. 14) into an ice-filled highball glass and stir in the club soda. Garnish with the remaining sage leaf and the twist.

hot buttered lemon

2 tablespoons unsalted butter

2 ounces fresh lemon juice

2 ounces hot water

½ ounce Simple Syrup (P. 16)

1 orange wedge

1 lemon wheel

Pinch of freshly grated nutmeg

Pinch of cinnamon

Reaburn loves lemon and butter together ("they're yummy and rich"), and this drink is one of his favorite incarnations of the pairing. "It's like a hot buttered rum mixed with a lemon tart. The citrus pieces get softened by the heat and mellowed by the sugar and butter; they're delicious to nibble on at the end of the drink." Reaburn sometimes varies the Hot Buttered Lemon by adding cloves and fresh ginger, which give it "a little zing."

In a small saucepan, melt the butter in the lemon juice over moderate heat. Add the hot water, Simple Syrup, orange wedge, lemon wheel, nutmeg and cinnamon and cook, stirring, until cloudy and hot. Pour into a small mug.

174

Hot Buttered Lemon

Minetta Burger, P. 202; Harvard Cooler, P. 34

Details, left to right: "Basso" plates by Calvin Klein; "Black and White" paper napkins by Paperproducts Design; glass by Nouvel Studio; "Family Tree" wallpaper by Ferm Living.

party food

spiced plantain chips

Nadine Waechter-Moreno • New York Bar, Tokyo

TOTAL: 30 MIN

6 SERVINGS

- 2 tablespoons sugar
- ½ teaspoon curry powder
- ½ teaspoon pimentón de la Vera (smoked Spanish paprika)
- ½ teaspoon salt

Pinch of cayenne pepper

Vegetable oil, for frying

- 3 firm, green plantains, peeled

Waechter-Moreno serves these cayenne-spiked chips at New York Bar alongside other snacks like truffled popcorn and tandoori-spiced cashews. To get perfectly thin plantain slices, she uses a meat slicer (a mandoline will work just as well).

1 In a small bowl, mix the sugar with the curry powder, smoked paprika, salt and cayenne pepper.

2 In a large, deep saucepan, heat 2 inches of vegetable oil to 350°. Slice the plantains 1/16 inch thick. Working in batches, fry the plantains, stirring occasionally, until golden and crisp, about 4 minutes. Using a slotted spoon, transfer the chips to paper towels to drain. Immediately sprinkle generously with the spice mix, toss to coat and serve.

party food

devils on horseback

Adam Penney • Chinawhite, London

ACTIVE: 20 MIN; TOTAL: 1 HR
PLUS OVERNIGHT MARINATING

6 SERVINGS

- ½ **cup Armagnac or Cognac**
- ½ **cup water**
- 2 **thyme sprigs plus**
  ½ teaspoon thyme
  leaves
- 2 **garlic cloves**
- 18 **pitted prunes**

Freshly ground pepper

- 18 **thin slices of pancetta**
  (about ¾ pound)

Extra-virgin olive oil,
  for drizzling

These sticky, sweet and salty snacks of prunes wrapped in pancetta remind Penney of his childhood, when his parents made them for "canapé parties." He put the 1970s-era appetizer on the menu at Chinawhite along with another classic, Angels on Horseback (bacon-wrapped oysters), and his own Demons on Horseback (venison carpaccio–wrapped prunes with a little bitter chocolate).

1 In a medium saucepan, combine the Armagnac with the water, thyme sprigs and garlic. Bring to a boil and remove from the heat. Add the prunes and season lightly with pepper. Let stand until cool, then cover and refrigerate overnight.
2 Preheat the oven to 375°. Remove the prunes from the soaking liquid and pat dry. Set a prune in the center of each pancetta slice. Sprinkle with the thyme leaves and season with pepper. Roll up the prunes in the pancetta and set the bundles seam side down on a parchment paper–lined baking sheet. Drizzle lightly with olive oil. Bake for about 15 minutes, until the prunes are hot and the pancetta is crisp. Serve with toothpicks.

chunky guacamole

Richard Sandoval • Ketsi, Punta Mita, Mexico

TOTAL: 20 MIN

4 TO 6 SERVINGS

- 3 Hass avocados, cut into ½-inch dice
- 1 plum tomato, seeded and finely diced
- ¼ cup finely diced onion
- 2 tablespoons minced cilantro
- 1 serrano chile, seeded and minced
- 1 tablespoon fresh lime juice

Kosher salt

Tortilla chips, for serving

Mexico City native Sandoval makes his guacamole tableside in a volcanic-rock molcajete (mortar and pestle) and serves it with hot, superthin corn tortilla chips and two kinds of salsa: avocado-and-tomatillo and fresh tomato.

In a medium bowl, gently stir the diced avocados with the tomato, onion, cilantro, chile and lime juice until well mixed but still slightly chunky. Season the guacamole with salt and serve with tortilla chips.

180

Chunky Guacamole and
Red Sangrita, P. 86

*"Loos" shot glass by Lobmeyr
from Neue Galerie.*

hand-cut fries with smoked aioli

Michael Paley • Proof on Main, Louisville, Kentucky

TOTAL: 1 HR

6 SERVINGS

- ¾ cup mayonnaise
- 1 garlic clove
- 1 teaspoon pimentón de la Vera (smoked Spanish paprika)
- 1 teaspoon fresh lemon juice
- 1 tablespoon plus 2 teaspoons finely chopped flat-leaf parsley

Kosher salt and freshly ground pepper

Vegetable oil, for frying

- 3 large baking potatoes (about 2 pounds), peeled and cut into ½-inch-thick sticks

These ultra-crispy fries are a favorite at Proof on Main, where Paley goes through roughly 500 Idaho potatoes a week making them. Use very firm potatoes to ensure optimum crispness.

1 In a food processor, puree the mayonnaise with the garlic, smoked paprika and lemon juice. Stir in 2 teaspoons of the parsley and season with salt and pepper. Scrape the aioli into a small bowl and refrigerate.

2 In a large saucepan, heat 1 inch of oil to 250°. In a large bowl, rinse the potatoes and pat thoroughly dry. Working in batches, fry the potatoes until they are almost tender and look dry on the outside, about 6 minutes. Transfer to paper towels to drain.

3 Increase the oil temperature to 350°. Cook the fries in batches until golden and crisp, about 3 minutes. Transfer to paper towels to drain and immediately season with salt. Sprinkle the fries with the remaining 1 tablespoon of parsley and serve with the smoked aioli.

Hand-Cut Fries
with Smoked Aioli

gougères

Christophe Michalak • Le Bar du Plaza Athénée, Paris

ACTIVE: 20 MIN; TOTAL: 1 HR

MAKES 4 DOZEN GOUGÈRES

- ¼ cup water
- 2 tablespoons unsalted butter
- 2 teaspoons dry white wine
- ½ teaspoon salt
- Pinch of freshly ground pepper
- ½ cup all-purpose flour
- 2 large eggs
- 3½ ounces Gruyère cheese, shredded (about 1¼ cups)

At the über-elegant Hôtel Plaza Athénée, pastry chef Michalak serves these diminutive cheese puffs to guests who order drinks at the bar.

1 Preheat the oven to 375°. In a medium saucepan, combine the water, butter, wine, salt and pepper and bring to a boil over moderate heat. Add the flour all at once and beat with a wooden spoon until the dough is smooth and gathers into a ball, about 1 minute. Remove from the heat and let stand until cooled slightly, about 5 minutes. Beat in 1 egg at a time, beating until the dough is smooth and slightly sticky between additions. Stir in the Gruyère.

2 Fit a pastry bag with a ½-inch tip and fill the bag with the dough. Pipe 1-inch mounds of the dough onto 2 parchment paper–lined baking sheets. Bake for about 30 minutes, until the cheese puffs are golden, rotating the baking sheets halfway through. Serve warm.

184

egg-and-potato tortilla

Maite Sabadell • Café de la Concha, San Sebastián, Spain

TOTAL: 35 MIN

6 TO 8 SERVINGS

- ¼ cup extra-virgin olive oil
- 2 medium Yukon Gold potatoes—peeled, halved lengthwise and cut crosswise into ½-inch-thick slices
- 1 large Spanish onion, halved and thinly sliced

Kosher salt

- 8 large eggs, lightly beaten

This traditional Spanish dish is made daily with all local ingredients at Sabadell's family-owned beachside restaurant. Sabadell also makes the tortilla for her grown children to eat on the plane when they travel.

1 Preheat the broiler. In a large nonstick ovenproof skillet, heat the olive oil. Add the potatoes and cook over moderate heat until almost tender, about 7 minutes. Add the onion and cook, stirring occasionally, until tender, about 8 minutes. Using the back of a wooden spoon, coarsely break up some of the potatoes and season with salt. Add the eggs and stir to combine. Cook until the eggs are set on the bottom and at the edge.

2 Transfer the skillet to the broiler and broil the tortilla about 2 inches from the heat for about 1½ minutes, until set and golden in spots. Invert the tortilla onto a serving plate, cut into wedges and serve warm or at room temperature.

croques meurice

Yannick Alléno • Bar 228, Paris

TOTAL: 55 MIN

8 SERVINGS

Sixteen 1½-inch cubes of crustless white Pullman bread

4 tablespoons unsalted butter, 2 tablespoons melted

2 tablespoons all-purpose flour

⅓ cup whole milk

4 ounces Comté or Gruyère cheese, shredded (1½ cups)

¼ cup finely diced baked ham

Pinch of freshly grated nutmeg

Kosher salt and freshly ground pepper

These bite-size ham-and-cheese sandwiches are miniature versions of the Croque Meurice that Michelin three-star chef Alléno serves exclusively at Le Meurice hotel's chic Bar 228.

1 Preheat the oven to 375°. Using kitchen scissors, cut a ½-inch square from the center of each bread cube; don't cut through the bottom. Discard the squares. In a bowl, toss the hollowed-out bread cubes with the 2 tablespoons of melted butter. Arrange the cubes on a baking sheet and bake for about 8 minutes, until they are lightly toasted.

2 Increase the oven temperature to 425°. In a small saucepan, melt the remaining 2 tablespoons of butter. Add the flour and cook over moderate heat, whisking, until smooth, about 1 minute. Whisk in the milk until a thick paste forms. Remove from the heat and fold in the cheese and ham. Season with the nutmeg, salt and pepper. Spoon the cheese filling into the bread cubes. Bake for about 5 minutes, until the cheese is melted. Serve hot.

186

Croques Meurice

Faux snakeskin tray by Two's Company from Global Table.

shrimp cocktail with marie rose sauce

Anthony Sedlak · The Corner Suite Bistro De Luxe, Vancouver

TOTAL: 20 MIN

4 SERVINGS

- ¼ cup mayonnaise
- 1 tablespoon ketchup
- 1 tablespoon fresh lemon juice
- 1 tablespoon snipped chives
- 2 teaspoons horseradish, preferably finely grated fresh
- ¼ teaspoon brandy

Kosher salt and freshly ground pepper

- 1 pound shelled and deveined cooked large shrimp
- 1 cup shredded iceberg lettuce
- 1 Hass avocado, thinly sliced
- 2 tablespoons canned fried onions

Toasted baguette slices, for serving

Chef and Food Network Canada star Sedlak spikes the '70s throwback Marie Rose sauce (mayonnaise and a touch of ketchup) with brandy and horseradish. It's fantastic with shrimp cocktail as well as fried seafood like battered cod.

1 In a large bowl, mix the mayonnaise with the ketchup, lemon juice, snipped chives, horseradish and brandy and season with salt and pepper. Add the shrimp and toss to coat.

2 Make a bed of the shredded lettuce on plates or in martini glasses. Top with the shrimp cocktail and arrange the avocado alongside. Garnish with the fried onions and serve with baguette toasts.

Shrimp Cocktail
with Marie Rose Sauce

*"Float" bowl by Molo from
Velocity Art and Design.*

grilled asparagus salad with fried eggs

Mark Broadbent • The East Room, London

TOTAL: 30 MIN

6 SERVINGS

- ¼ cup extra-virgin olive oil
- 1 tablespoon fresh lemon juice
- 1 teaspoon Dijon mustard

Kosher salt and freshly ground pepper

- 1 pound medium asparagus, trimmed
- 2 tablespoons unsalted butter
- 6 large eggs
- 6 cups baby arugula
- ¾ cup freshly shaved Parmigiano-Reggiano cheese (about 2½ ounces)

Chef Broadbent upgrades the standard lemony arugula salad by topping it with grilled asparagus, butter-fried eggs— duck eggs, when available—and freshly shaved Parmigiano-Reggiano.

1 In a small bowl, whisk 3 tablespoons of the olive oil with the lemon juice and mustard. Season with salt and pepper.

2 Light a grill or preheat a grill pan. In a large bowl, toss the asparagus with the remaining 1 tablespoon of olive oil and season with salt and pepper. Grill the asparagus over high heat until tender and charred in spots, about 5 minutes; keep warm.

3 Meanwhile, in a large nonstick skillet, melt the butter over moderate heat. Working in batches if necessary, cook the eggs sunny-side up until the whites are firm and the yolks runny, about 5 minutes. Season with salt and pepper.

4 In a bowl, toss the arugula with the lemon vinaigrette and transfer the salad to plates. Top with the asparagus, fried eggs and cheese shavings and serve at once.

Grilled Asparagus Salad
with Fried Egg

*"Ripple" tray by 3,co
for Urban Oasis.*

spiced seafood skewers

Steve Baker • Mesa & Manifesto, Shanghai

TOTAL: 30 MIN

4 SERVINGS

- 1½ teaspoons yellow mustard seeds
- 1 teaspoon black peppercorns
- ¾ teaspoon chile powder
- 1 small bay leaf
- ½ teaspoon celery seeds
- ½ teaspoon coriander seeds
- ¼ teaspoon ground ginger
- 1½ tablespoons kosher salt
- 12 large shrimp, shelled and deveined
- 8 large sea scallops
- ¾ pound salmon fillet with skin, cut into 8 cubes
- 2 tablespoons extra-virgin olive oil
- 1 tablespoon minced flat-leaf parsley

Lemon wedges, for serving

Baker features these skewers on Manifesto's outdoor terrace during their summer Sunday "DJ & BBQ sessions." In place of salmon or scallops you can substitute tuna, sea bass, marlin or swordfish.

1 In a small skillet, combine the mustard seeds, peppercorns, chile powder, bay leaf, celery seeds, coriander seeds and ginger and stir over moderate heat until fragrant, about 2 minutes. Transfer to a spice grinder and let cool completely, then grind to a powder. Stir in the salt.
2 Light a grill or preheat a grill pan. Thread the shrimp onto 4 metal skewers. Alternate the scallops and salmon cubes on 4 more metal skewers. Brush the skewers with the olive oil and season generously with the spice mix. (Reserve any remaining spice mix for another use.)
3 Grill the skewers over moderately high heat until the seafood is lightly charred and just cooked through, about 4 minutes. Sprinkle the seafood with the parsley and serve with lemon wedges.

lemongrass chicken wings

Anthony Herzog • Seamstress, Melbourne

ACTIVE: 45 MIN; TOTAL: 5 HR
PLUS OVERNIGHT MARINATING

4 SERVINGS

- 4 cups water
- 3 tablespoons sugar
- 3 tablespoons salt
- 2 pounds chicken wings, split at the joints, wing tips discarded
- 2 scallions, thinly sliced
- 1 long, red chile, such as Holland, seeded and finely chopped

One 1-inch piece of fresh ginger, peeled and finely chopped

- 1 lemongrass stalk, tender inner white part only, finely chopped
- ½ cup vegetable oil, plus more for frying
- 1 cup tapioca flour mixed with 1 teaspoon baking soda, or 1 cup cornstarch
- 1 tablespoon chopped cilantro

Lime wedges, for serving

For this spicy, sweet and salty riff on fried chicken wings, the all-American bar snack, Herzog uses ingredients from his local Asian market, including ginger, chile, lemongrass and lime. The wings are fabulous with margaritas.

1 In a medium saucepan, heat the water, sugar and salt, stirring, until dissolved. Let cool. In a large bowl, pour the brine over the chicken wings. Cover and refrigerate for 4 hours; drain and pat dry.
2 Meanwhile, in a large heatproof bowl, combine the scallions, chile, ginger and lemongrass. In a small saucepan, heat the ½ cup of oil until almost smoking. Pour the hot oil over the scallion mixture and let stand until cooled. Add the wings, toss to coat and refrigerate overnight.
3 In a large saucepan, heat 2 inches of oil to 350°. Drain the wings. In a medium bowl, toss the wings in the tapioca flour mixture until well coated. Fry the wings in batches until golden and cooked through, about 7 minutes per batch. Drain on paper towels, sprinkle with the cilantro and serve with lime wedges.

mussels with black bean and chile sauce

Neil Perry • Spice Temple, Sydney

TOTAL: 30 MIN

4 SERVINGS

- ¼ cup peanut oil
- 1 onion, halved and thinly sliced
- One 1-inch piece of fresh ginger, peeled and cut into thin matchsticks
- 1 tablespoon fermented black beans
- ½ teaspoon Asian ground chiles in oil or crushed red pepper
- 2 tablespoons Chinese black vinegar
- 2 pounds mussels, scrubbed and debearded
- 1 scallion, thinly sliced

Australian star chef Perry loves the complex combination of Asian flavors in this dish: salty fermented beans, hot chiles and sweet, briny mussels.

1 In a large wok, heat 2 tablespoons of the peanut oil. Add the onion and ginger and stir-fry over high heat until golden, about 5 minutes. Scrape into a mortar and add the black beans and ground chiles. Mash until coarsely ground. Stir in the vinegar. 2 Heat the remaining 2 tablespoons of peanut oil in the wok. Add the black bean mixture and stir-fry over moderate heat until fragrant, about 1 minute. Add the mussels, cover and steam until they open, about 4 minutes; discard any mussels that don't open. Transfer the mussels and sauce to a large bowl, sprinkle with the sliced scallion and serve hot.

Mussels with Black Bean and Chile Sauce
and One Hot Minute, P. 88

"Verona" glass (right) by Nouvel Studio.

fried pork cutlet sandwiches

Shinya Ikeda • D-Heartman, Tokyo

TOTAL: 30 MIN

4 SERVINGS

- 4 pork cutlets (about 1 pound)
- Kosher salt and freshly ground pepper
- ¼ cup all-purpose flour
- 1 large egg, beaten
- 1¼ cups *panko* (Japanese bread crumbs)
- Vegetable oil, for frying
- 2 tablespoons unsalted butter, softened
- 8 slices of white sandwich bread
- ¼ cup *tonkatsu* sauce
- Dill pickles, for serving (optional)

*Breaded, deep-fried pork cutlets (*tonkatsu*) are wildly popular in Japan. The tangy, apple-and-tomato-based sauce that accompanies them—sometimes referred to as Japanese Worcestershire sauce—is also known as* tonkatsu. *Kikkoman makes a good version, which is available at Asian food stores and pacificeastwest.com.*

1 Season the pork cutlets with salt and pepper. Put the flour, egg and *panko* into 3 separate shallow bowls. Dust the cutlets with the flour, then dip them into the egg and coat with the *panko*, pressing lightly to help the crumbs adhere.

2 In a large skillet, heat ¼ inch of oil until shimmering. Fry the cutlets 2 at a time over high heat, turning once, until golden and crisp, about 3 minutes. Transfer to paper towels to drain.

3 Lightly butter the bread and top with the fried pork cutlets. Spoon the *tonkatsu* sauce on top of the cutlets and close the sandwiches. Cut into thirds and serve with dill pickles.

steak-and-chorizo empanadas

Guillermo Gonzalez • The Parrot Club, San Juan, Puerto Rico

TOTAL: 1 HR

10 SERVINGS

- 4 ounces dry Spanish chorizo, cut into ½-inch dice
- ¼ cup finely diced red bell pepper
- ¼ cup finely diced Italian frying pepper
- ¼ cup finely diced onion
- 1 small garlic clove, minced
- ½ pound skirt steak, cut into ½-inch dice
- Kosher salt and freshly ground pepper
- ½ cup shredded Monterey Jack cheese
- 2 tablespoons finely chopped cilantro
- Ten 5-inch empanada wrappers, such as Goya, thawed if frozen
- Vegetable oil, for frying
- 1 cup sour cream mixed with 1 tablespoon fresh lemon juice and ¼ cup minced cilantro, for serving

Gonzalez loves mojitos with these spicy and rich empanadas. At home, he sometimes substitutes a mixture of mayonnaise, ketchup, Tabasco, garlic and cilantro for the cilantro cream here.

1 In a large skillet, cook the chorizo over moderate heat until the fat has rendered, about 4 minutes. Using a slotted spoon, transfer the chorizo to a bowl. Drain off all but 1 tablespoon of the fat. Add the peppers, onion and garlic and cook until tender, about 5 minutes. Add the steak and chorizo and cook until the steak is no longer pink, about 3 minutes. Season with salt and pepper and transfer to a bowl to cool. Stir in the cheese and cilantro.
2 Arrange the empanada wrappers on a work surface. Spoon the filling onto the bottom half of each round and fold the top over. Crimp the edges with a fork to seal the empanadas.
3 In a large, deep skillet, heat ½ inch of oil to 350°. Fry the empanadas in batches, turning once, until golden all over, about 3 minutes per batch. Transfer to paper towels to drain. Serve the empanadas with the cilantro–sour cream dipping sauce.

kogi dogs

Roy Choi • Kogi, Los Angeles

TOTAL: 40 MIN

8 SERVINGS

- 2 cups finely shredded green cabbage
- 1 large scallion, finely chopped
- 1 tablespoon fresh lime juice

Salt and freshly ground pepper

- ½ cup mayonnaise
- 1 tablespoon toasted sesame seeds, crushed
- 1 tablespoon vegetable oil, plus more for brushing
- 1 cup kimchi, drained and patted dry
- 8 hot dog buns
- 8 all-beef hot dogs, partially split
- 1 cup shredded sharp cheddar cheese
- 2 cups shredded romaine lettuce
- 1 small onion, thinly sliced
- 2 cups cilantro sprigs

Sriracha sauce, for drizzling

These kimchi-topped dogs with cilantro and cheddar are Choi's Korean-Mexican spin on L.A.'s famous dirty dog, a bacon-wrapped hot dog with fried peppers and onions. He serves the dogs at the Culver City bar Alibi Room as well as from his Korean taco trucks, announcing their locations on Twitter.

1 In a large bowl, toss the cabbage with the scallion and lime juice; season with salt and pepper. In a small bowl, mix the mayonnaise with the sesame seeds and season with salt.

2 In a nonstick skillet, heat the 1 tablespoon of oil. Add the kimchi and cook over high heat until browned, about 3 minutes.

3 Light a grill or preheat a grill pan. Brush the cut sides of the buns with oil and grill over moderately high heat until toasted on both sides, about 45 seconds total. Spread the cut sides with the sesame mayonnaise.

4 Grill the hot dogs over moderately high heat until nicely charred all over. Tuck the hot dogs into the buns and top with the kimchi, cheddar, cabbage salad, lettuce, onion and cilantro. Drizzle with Sriracha and serve.

198

Kogi Dog and Gone Native, P. 74

Glass by Nouvel Studio.

bbq pulled-pork sandwiches

David Chang • Momofuku Ssäm Bar, Manhattan

ACTIVE: 45 MIN;
TOTAL: 5 HR 15 MIN

8 SERVINGS

One 5-pound boneless pork shoulder, cut in half

Kosher salt and freshly ground pepper

½ cup tomato paste

1½ teaspoons hot paprika

¼ teaspoon ground cloves

¼ teaspoon ground allspice

½ cup packed dark brown sugar

1 cup cider vinegar

¼ cup molasses

1 cup ketchup

1 tablespoon ground coffee (not instant)

1 cup water

8 brioche buns, split

Coleslaw, for serving

Chang likes eating these vinegary, spicy sandwiches late at night with a mint julep.

1 Season the pork with salt and pepper. Heat a large cast-iron casserole. Add the pork, fat side down, and cook over moderately high heat until browned all over, about 12 minutes total. Transfer to a plate. Add the tomato paste to the casserole and cook over moderately low heat, stirring, until deep red, 2 minutes. Add the paprika, cloves, allspice and brown sugar and cook until the sugar dissolves, about 30 seconds. Add the vinegar and bring to a boil, scraping up any browned bits. Add the molasses, ketchup, ground coffee and water and bring to a simmer.

2 Return the pork to the casserole. Cover and cook over low heat, turning the pork in the sauce occasionally, until very tender, about 4 hours. Transfer the pork to a large bowl; let rest for 30 minutes.

3 Meanwhile, skim the fat from the sauce. Boil the sauce over moderately high heat until thickened slightly, about 5 minutes. Using 2 forks, shred the pork; discard any large pieces of fat. Stir the shredded pork into the barbecue sauce. Mound the pork on the buns, top with coleslaw and serve.

200

lamb and blue cheese french dip

Jason Gancedo • Cole's, Los Angeles

ACTIVE: 40 MIN;
TOTAL: 3 HR 15 MIN

4 SERVINGS

- 2 garlic cloves
- 1 teaspoon fresh rosemary
- 1 teaspoon thyme leaves

Kosher salt and freshly ground pepper

- 2 pounds lamb shoulder, cut into 3-inch chunks
- 1 tablespoon vegetable oil
- 2 cups beef stock or low-sodium broth
- ½ teaspoon Worcestershire sauce
- ¼ teaspoon dark brown sugar
- 4 French rolls, split and lightly toasted

Dijon mustard (optional)

- 2 ounces Maytag blue cheese, crumbled

Cole's is the self-proclaimed originator of the French Dip, a hot sandwich typically made with generous amounts of roast beef on a French roll and served au jus. Gancedo serves his sandwich with a superhot, house-cured Atomic Pickle Spear.

1 Preheat the oven to 250°. In a mini food processor, chop the garlic. Add the rosemary, thyme, 2 teaspoons of kosher salt and a pinch of pepper and process until the herbs are finely chopped. Rub the lamb all over with the herb salt.

2 In an enameled cast-iron casserole, heat the oil. Add the lamb and cook over high heat until lightly browned all over, about 8 minutes. Add the stock and bring to a boil. Cover and braise in the oven for about 2½ hours, until the lamb is very tender. Transfer the lamb to a bowl and let rest for 5 minutes. Strain the cooking liquid and skim off the fat. Season the jus with the Worcestershire sauce, brown sugar and salt and pepper; keep warm.

3 Shred the lamb, discarding any large pieces of fat. Spread the rolls with mustard and top with the lamb and blue cheese. Serve the jus alongside.

minetta burger

Lee Hanson & Riad Nasr • Minetta Tavern, Manhattan

TOTAL: 1 HR 15 MIN

4 SERVINGS

- 2 tablespoons unsalted butter
- 1 large yellow onion, halved and thinly sliced
- ¼ cup water
- Kosher salt and freshly ground pepper
- 2 pounds ground sirloin
- 1 tablespoon vegetable oil
- 5 ounces sharp cheddar cheese, thinly sliced
- 4 brioche buns, split and toasted
- Lettuce, tomato slices and pickles, for serving

Minetta Tavern has become known for its spectacular hamburgers. The restaurant's namesake burger is made with a blend of beef short rib and brisket from the nearly century-old local purveyor Pat La Frieda.

1 In a large skillet, melt the butter. Add the onion and cook over moderate heat, stirring occasionally, until deep golden, about 40 minutes. Add the water and scrape up any browned bits. Cook until the liquid evaporates, about 5 minutes. Season the caramelized onion with salt and pepper; keep warm.

2 Gently shape the sirloin into four 1-inch-thick patties. Season generously with salt and pepper. In a large cast-iron skillet, heat the oil. Cook the burgers over moderately high heat until deep brown outside and medium-rare within, about 6 minutes per side. During the last 2 minutes, top the burgers with the cheese and cover loosely with foil so the cheese melts. Transfer the burgers to the buns, top with the caramelized onion and serve with a side of lettuce, tomato and pickles.

rib eyes with crispy potatoes and chimichurri

Martin Arrieta • Gran Bar Danzon, Buenos Aires

ACTIVE: 25 MIN; TOTAL: 50 MIN

2 SERVINGS

- 1 garlic clove
- ¾ cup lightly packed flat-leaf parsley leaves
- 1 tablespoon oregano leaves
- 2 teaspoons thyme leaves

Leaves from one 2½-inch rosemary sprig

- 6 sage leaves
- ¼ teaspoon crushed red pepper
- ¼ cup extra-virgin olive oil

Kosher salt and freshly ground pepper

Two ½-pound boneless rib eye steaks

Vegetable oil, for frying

- 2 medium baking potatoes (about 1 pound)—boiled, peeled and cut into 1-inch chunks

The industrial-chic Gran Bar Danzon always has a rib eye steak on its menu. This delicious and straightforward version is served with a bright chimichurri sauce and crisp-tender roasted potatoes.

1 In a food processor, pulse the garlic until finely chopped. Add the parsley, oregano, thyme, rosemary, sage and crushed red pepper and pulse until the herbs are finely chopped. Add the olive oil and pulse to blend. Season with salt and pepper and transfer the chimichurri to a bowl.
2 Light a grill or heat a grill pan. Season the steaks with salt and pepper and grill over moderately high heat, turning once, until well browned outside and medium-rare within, about 10 minutes total. Let rest for 5 minutes.
3 Meanwhile, in a medium saucepan, heat 1 inch of vegetable oil to 350°. Fry the potatoes in batches until golden and crisp, about 4 minutes per batch. Using a slotted spoon, transfer the potatoes to paper towels to drain. Season with salt. Serve the steaks with the potatoes and chimichurri.

top 100 bars worldwide

UNITED STATES

ATLANTA Holeman & Finch Public House This gastropub co-owned by mixologist Greg Best serves offbeat cocktails such as the Johnny Ryall (Angostura bitters, cherry liqueur and Miller High Life). *2277 Peachtree Rd.; 404-948-1175; holeman-finch.com.*

BOSTON Drink Star chef Barbara Lynch's bar dispenses with menus; mixologist John Gertsen and his crew—including Misty Kalkofen, who created Her Majesty's Pearl (P. 152)—custom-make drinks for each customer. *348 Congress St.; 617-695-1806; drinkfortpoint.com.*

BOSTON Eastern Standard Kitchen & Drinks Jackson Cannon presides over Eastern Standard's 46-foot-long marble-topped bar (and the menu of 50-plus drinks) in Kenmore Square's elegant Hotel Commonwealth. *528 Commonwealth Ave.; 617-532-9100.*

CHICAGO The Drawing Room At this subterranean lounge within Le Passage nightclub, guests can have their drinks prepared tableside from a custom-made bar cart, accompanied by a cocktail history lesson. *937 N. Rush St.; 312-266-2694; lepassage.com.*

CHICAGO Nacional 27 Adam Seger (whose namesake drink is on P. 52) makes the terrific cocktails at this salsa club and restaurant. Seger recently came out with his own hibiscus-infused Hum liqueur. *325 W. Huron St.; 312-664-2727; nacional27.net.*

CHICAGO The Violet Hour With chandeliers and a fireplace, this lounge is modeled after early-19th-century English clubs and French salons. Floor-to-ceiling curtains frame the bartenders as if they were on a stage. Snacks include fried peanut butter–banana bites with and bacon. *1520 N. Damen Ave.; 773-252-1500; theviolethour.com.*

HOUSTON Anvil Bar & Refuge A group of self-described cocktail freaks serves old-school drinks from an extra-long bar at this former Firestone tire shop. *1424 Westheimer Rd.; 713-523-1622; anvilhouston.com.*

LAS VEGAS Parasol Down Lush landscaping and a waterfall are part of the draw at this Wynn Las Vegas indoor/outdoor lounge. As for the drinks, there are twists on classics (like cucumber collinses) plus more unusual choices like Chestnut Butter Rum. *3131 Las Vegas Blvd. S.; 877-321-9966.*

LAS VEGAS Petrossian Bar In addition to live music from a Steinway grand, this opulent, Old World–style bar in the lobby of the Bellagio features a dizzying selection of vodkas (which servers can match with just the right caviar). *3600 Las Vegas Blvd. S.; 888-987-6667.*

LOS ANGELES The Doheny A trio of bar luminaries—Vincenzo Marianella, Eric Alperin and Seven Grand alum Marcos Tello—create the constantly changing cocktail list for this members-only club inside a former greenhouse. *714 W. Olympic Blvd.; no phone; thedoheny.com.*

LOS ANGELES The Edison Andrew Meieran's crew serves handcrafted cocktails, an amazing gin selection and snacks like bacon-maple beer nuts at this lounge inside an old power plant. *108 W. Second St.; 213-613-0000; edisondowntown.com.*

LOS ANGELES Seven Grand In addition to bourbon-based creations like John Coltharp's Honey & Spice (P. 158), this swank Irish pub offers 271 whiskeys and Maker's Mark–dipped cigars. *515 W. Seventh St.; 213-614-0737.*

LOS ANGELES The Varnish A collaboration between Cedd Moses and cocktail magnates Sasha Petraske and Eric Alperin, The Varnish is accessible only through a secret door at Cole's, the destination French Dip restaurant. *118 E. Sixth St.; 213-622-9999; thevarnishbar.com.*

MIAMI BEACH The Florida Room The center of Miami Beach nightlife, Lenny Kravitz's updated 1950s Cuban–style lounge in the Delano has music played on a Lucite grand piano and over 30 Latin-inspired drinks. *1685 Collins Ave.; 305-674-6152; delano-hotel.com.*

NEW ORLEANS Arnaud's French 75 Bar Chris Hannah, who created the ginger-spiked Thamyris (P. 151), mans the bar at this dapper, cigar-friendly spot inside Arnaud's, one of New Orleans's oldest and most venerated restaurants. *813 Bienville St.; 866-230-8895; arnauds.com.*

NEW ORLEANS Cure Bartenders at this newcomer use droppers to add house-made tinctures to their cocktails, and chef Jason McCullar seasons his "Pincho" ribs with Angostura bitters. *4905 Freret St.; 504-302-2357; curenola.com.*

NEW YORK CITY B Flat This subterranean lounge has live jazz, great Japanese-accented small plates and sake-based cocktails named after jazz classics like John Coltrane's "Giant Steps" (wasabi-infused vodka and *junmai daiginjo* sake). *277 Church St., Manhattan; 212-219-2970; bflat.info.*

NEW YORK CITY Clover Club Named after a pre-Prohibition men's club whose members met to eat, drink and heckle guests of honor, this classic-cocktails spot is co-owned by Julie Reiner of Manhattan's renowned Flatiron Lounge. *210 Smith St., Brooklyn; 718-855-7939; cloverclubny.com.*

NEW YORK CITY Death & Co. *Food & Wine Cocktails* deputy editor Joaquin Simo and the other vest-clad bartenders at this East Village spot have an encyclopedic knowledge of cocktails. Offerings include Simo's famous tequila-and-mezcal-spiked Smoked Horchata. *433 E. Sixth St., Manhattan; 212-388-0882; deathandcompany.com.*

NEW YORK CITY Dutch Kills Modeled after an 1890s "gentlemen's tavern," this bar from local-hero mixologist Richard Boccato serves classic cocktails made with hand-cut ice and features live music throughout the week. *27-24 Jackson Ave., Long Island City; 718-383-2724; dutchkillsbar.com.*

NEW YORK CITY Little Branch At this subterranean lounge owned by Milk & Honey's Sasha Petraske and cocktail expert Joseph Schwartz, a nattily dressed staff mixes drinks with ice custom-made for each glass. *20 Seventh Ave. S., Manhattan; 212-929-4360; littlebranch.net.*

NEW YORK CITY Mayahuel Death & Co. alum Philip Ward opened this East Village Mexican spot in 2009 with food by Luis Gonzales and a cocktail menu dedicated to tequila and mezcal. *304 E. Sixth St., Manhattan; 212-253-5888; mayahuelny.com.*

NEW YORK CITY PDT Mixologist Jim Meehan, deputy editor of *Food & Wine Cocktails*, obsesses over obscure classic drinks at this excellent reservations-only lounge. The (unmarked) door is in a phone booth inside the hot dog joint Crif Dogs. *113 St. Marks Pl., Manhattan; 212-614-0386; pdtnyc.com.*

NEW YORK CITY Pegu Club Audrey Saunders, a leader of the vintage cocktail movement, co-owns this mixologists' hangout, which serves its drinks with dropper bottles of fresh juices, bitters and simple syrup. *77 W. Houston St., Manhattan; 212-473-7348; peguclub.com.*

PORTLAND, OR Beaker & Flask This restaurant and bar from Kevin Ludwig serves inspired cocktails like the Paul Revere (bourbon, bianco vermouth and Pinot Noir grenadine) alongside seasonal dishes like maple-braised pork belly.

206

720 SE Sandy Blvd.; 503-235-8180; beakerandflask.com.

PORTLAND, OR Clyde Common Jeffrey Morgenthaler oversees the rotating cocktail list at this airy industrial "tavern." One to try: the Yellowjacket, with 12-year-old rum, lime, house-made orange bitters and lavender-honey syrup. *1014 SW Stark St.; 503-228-3333; clydecommon.com.*

PORTLAND, OR Teardrop Cocktail Lounge The bartenders at Teardrop's circular bar make their own bitters, tonic water and specialty liqueurs for drinks like the Need for Tweed (Scotch, absinthe, malted pumpkin and chipotle-chocolate bitters). *1015 NW Everett St.; 503-445-8109; teardroplounge.com.*

SAN FRANCISCO The Alembic This gastropub offers a terrific list of "After-Dinner Libations" like brandies and Scotches and "Daytime" drinks like mint juleps. *1725 Haight St.; 415-666-0822; alembicbar.com.*

SAN FRANCISCO Beretta An upscale pizzeria with communal seating and a late-night cocktail lounge, Beretta serves fantastic drinks like the Dolores Park Swizzle (rum, lime, maraschino, absinthe, bitters). *1199 Valencia St.; 415-695-1199; berettasf.com.*

SAN FRANCISCO Heaven's Dog This northern Chinese restaurant and bar from chef Charles Phan of the Slanted Door offers a dozen or so classically influenced cocktails from mixologist Erik Adkins, like the Cap Haitian Rum & Honey (made with local honey). *1148 Mission St.; 415-863-6008; heavensdog.com.*

SAN FRANCISCO Rickhouse The newest place from the owners of Bourbon & Branch, Rickhouse specializes in whiskey and punches (including a gingery Pimm's punch with gin and lemon) that are served with giant blocks of fruit-studded ice. *246 Kearny St.; 415-398-2827; rickhousebar.com.*

SEATTLE Vessel Cocktail aesthetes come to this elegant, modern bar in a renovated 1920s building for swizzles, flips and other drinks served over five different sizes of ice. *1312 Fifth Ave.; 206-652-0521; vesselseattle.com.*

SEATTLE Zig Zag Café This bartender-owned restaurant and bar near Pike Place Market serves forgotten drinks based on old cocktail recipes, like the White Lion (rum, lemon juice, falernum and bitters). *1501 Western Ave.; 206-625-1146; zigzagseattle.com.*

SEATTLE AREA The Naga Cocktail Lounge Drinks from the "Slings and Tikis" section of the menu at this bar inside an upscale Thai restaurant come in huge skull-shaped bowls—for $25—if you tell the bartender to "make it Brock Samson." (Brock is the larger-than-life bodyguard on the animated TV show *The Venture Bros.*) *601 108th Ave. NE, Bellevue, WA; 425-455-3226.*

ST. LOUIS Taste by Niche This small-plates and classic-minded-cocktails joint from Gerard Craft (an F&W Best New Chef 2008) features drinks by Ted Kilgore and snacks like house-made pickles and spicy pork meatballs. *1831 Sidney St.; 314-773-7755; nichestlouis.com.*

WASHINGTON, DC The Gibson This low-key but exclusive bar has an impressive list of well-crafted cocktails, both classic and innovative (like a celery-infused pisco sour). The waitstaff flames twists over drinks tableside. *2009 14th St. NW; 202-232-2156; thegibsondc.com.*

WASHINGTON, DC AREA PX Mixologist Todd Thrasher makes the cocktails—as well as seasonal bitters and tonic water—at this chandelier-lit speakeasy (there's no sign outside, just a blue light). It's owned by the team behind the terrific Restaurant Eve. *728 King St., Alexandria, VA; 703-299-8385.*

CANADA

TORONTO BarChef Mixologist Frankie Solarik mans the bar at this avant-garde lounge, where he serves classic as well as "molecular" creations like the Burnt Chartreuse (brandy, burnt Chartreuse, smoke essence and vanilla syrup "ravioli"). *472 Queen St. W.; 416-868-4800; barcheftoronto.com.*

VANCOUVER The Diamond The drink menu at this bar from three of Vancouver's craft-cocktail pioneers is divided into categories like "Boozy," "Proper" and "Delicate." For eating, there are Asian-inspired "Smaller" and "Bigger" plates. *6 Powell St.; no phone; di6mond.com.*

VANCOUVER George Head bartender Shaun Layton mixes stellar classic cocktails and original ones like the Mumbai Sling (gin, coriander, house-made ginger syrup and mango puree) at this stylish lounge with red leather banquettes and a glowing onyx bar top. *1137 Hamilton St.; 604-628-5555; georgelounge.com.*

VANCOUVER Pourhouse This cozy Gastown saloon offers hearty dishes like Welsh rarebit and a short but substantial list of drinks such as the Gold

Fashioned (bourbon, maple syrup, bitters and citrus zest). *162 Water St.; 604-568-7022; pourhousevancouver.com.*

MEXICO

GUADALAJARA

I Latina This colorful restaurant and bar in a renovated warehouse serves great riffs on south-of-the-border-style cocktails (tamarind margaritas) and a delectable food menu (coffee-crusted steak). A few doors away, the hip lunch spot Anita li (I Latina spelled backward) has terrific mojitos and Piña Lis (vodka, basil and pineapple). *Av. Inglaterra 3128; 011-52-33-3647-7774.*

SOUTH AMERICA

CUZCO, PERU

El Pisquerito Hans Hilburg, who created the minty Cholo Fresco (P. 152), owns this pisco-centric tapas bar in the ancient Incan capital. He uses only boutique and artisanal piscos, claiming that the South American spirit is "magical." *Calle San Juan de Dios 250; 011-51-84-23-5223; elpisquerito.com.*

LIMA **Malabar** Chef-owner Pedro Miguel Schiaffino serves homey dishes like goat braised in *chicha* (a fermented corn drink) and updated South American cocktails such as pisco punch with pineapple syrup and diced fresh pineapple. *Camino Real 101; 011-51-1-440-5200.*

LIMA **Maury Bar**
This early-1900s hotel in the historic center of Lima is rumored to be the birthplace of the pisco sour. *Ucayali 201; 011-51-1-428-8188.*

RIO DE JANEIRO
Academia da Cachaça
Stocked with scores of artisanal cachaças, this colorful indoor/outdoor bar in Rio's upscale Leblon neighborhood has served its famous *feijoada* (a meat and bean stew) for 25 years. *Rua Conde Bernadotte 26; 011-55-21-2529-2680.*

RIO DE JANEIRO **Baretto-Londra** Part of a luxe Ipanema hotel, this bar designed by Philippe Starck is a tribute to London's bygone rock-and-roll scene. Guests lounge in leather club chairs while admiring framed vintage British LPs. *Fasano Rio de Janeiro, Av. Vieira Souto 80; 011-55-21-3202-4000; fasano.com.br.*

SÃO PAULO **Bar Astor**
White wall tiles and lots of mirrors give this Vila Madalena neighborhood bar a bohemian vibe. Excellent classic cocktails are served as well as caipirinhas made with fresh seasonal fruit. *Rua Delfina 163; 011-55-11-3815-1364; barastor.com.br.*

EUROPE

AMSTERDAM Door 74 Philip Duff, who contributed the recipes for the Vodka, Aquavit & Genever chapter (P. 54), launched this beautifully appointed spot in a former garage. Old-school techniques and glassware complement seasonal drinks like the Cherry Flipside (raisin-infused Armagnac and cherry liqueur). *Reguliersdwarsstraat 74; 011-31-6-3404-5122.*

BARCELONA Dry Martini This swank bar has a secret restaurant in back (entered only with a constantly changing password) and a menu with a dozen variations on its namesake drink, like a wasabi-infused martini. *Carrer Aribau 162; 011-34-93-217-5080; drymartinibcn.com.*

BARCELONA Ideal Cocktail Bar Oil paintings and a dark wood bar decorate this old-school spot, which was opened in 1931 by current owner Josep Maria Gotarda's father. In addition to classics like Singapore Slings and mint juleps, Ideal claims to have the largest whisky selection in Europe. *Aribau 89; 011-34-93-453-1028; idealcocktailbar.com.*

BELFAST, IRELAND The Bar at the Merchant Hotel Sean Muldoon, who contributed the recipes for the Whiskey chapter (P. 108), makes precise cocktails at this opulent Victorian salon–style pub. The Connoisseurs Club (co-founded by Muldoon) meets here monthly to sample and discuss new and out-of-the-ordinary spirits. *35-39 Waring St.; 011-44-28-9023-4888; themerchanthotel.com.*

BERLIN Becketts Kopf Marked outside by an illuminated picture of Samuel Beckett's head (*Kopf* means "head"), this bar serves modernized drinks like the Lusitanian (aged Portuguese brandy and sweet vermouth). The menu is printed in copies of a book about the Irish writer. *Pappelallee 64; 011-49-162-237-9418.*

BERLIN Rum Trader Gregor Scholl is the bow-tied proprietor of this cozy bar—one of Berlin's oldest—with a huge rum selection. Scholl specializes in classic cocktails; he'll greet customers with the question *"Herb oder suess?"* (Tart or sweet?). *Fasanenstrasse 40; 011-49-30-8811-428.*

BRATISLAVA, SLOVAKIA Paparazzi Cocktail Bar & Ristorante Mixologist Stanislav Vadrna is an expert at the famous Japanese "hard shake." (His Masataka Swizzle is on P. 157.) He's made this modern Italian restaurant a destination in Eastern Europe. *Laurinská 1; 011-42-1-25-464-7971.*

top 100 bars worldwide

COPENHAGEN 1105 Bar Winner of the 2009 Copenhagen Cocktail Contest (entries had to contain cherry Heering, a Danish liqueur), Gromit Eduardsen creates the drinks at this beautifully designed, understated bar. The sound track: Motown and jazz. *Kristen Bernikows Gade 4; 011-45-3393-1105; 1105.dk.*

COPENHAGEN Nimb Bar Star mixologist Angus Winchester, who contributed the recipes for the Gin chapter (P. 68), helped launch the minimalist-Baroque Nimb hotel bar; it's decorated with chandeliers and a fireplace. *Bernstorffsgade 5; 011-45-8870-0000.*

COPENHAGEN Ruby The inconspicuous Ruby looks more like an elegant apartment than a bar. Bar manager Nick Kobbernagel turns out compelling drinks like the Genever Blush (P. 153) and the Carrot Head (gin, fresh carrot juice, Tabasco, ginger, coriander and honey). *Nybrogade 10; 011-45-3393-1203; rby.dk.*

EDINBURGH The Bon Vivant Stuart McCluskey (whose Auld Alliance is on P. 116) renovated this longtime New Town watering hole, but it retains a charmingly faded look (green marble tables, low lighting) and serves excellent drinks to match. The Tea Lady Fizz combines club soda with tea-infused gin. *55 Thistle St.; 011-44-131-225-3275; bonvivantedinburgh.co.uk.*

EDINBURGH Bramble Bar & Lounge A DJ booth and a framed concert poster of the Beastie Boys mix with tufted leather wing chairs at this edgy lounge. Drinks include excellent combinations like the Gin 'n' Jam (gin, rose petal jam and mint). *16A Queen St.; 011-44-131-226-6343; bramblebar.co.uk.*

EDINBURGH The Voodoo Rooms This sprawling, Belle Epoque–inspired restaurant, bar and live-music venue has an extensive collection of tequilas and rums and innovative cocktails like the Cash Jar (cachaça, rock candy, bitters and house-made ginger jam). *19a W. Register St.; 011-44-131-556-7060; thevoodoorooms.com.*

HAMBURG Le Lion At his intimate, über-refined bar, Jörg Meyer shows off his vast knowledge of cocktails with Soren Krogh, who created the pear-accented, sherry-based Klara Friis (P. 153). *Rathausstrasse 3; 011-49-40-3347-5378-0; lelion.net.*

HELSINKI A21 Cocktail Lounge Riffs on obscure classics like the Blinker (grapefruit juice, rye and raspberry syrup) and cocktails made with traditional Finnish flavors make up A21's drink menu. The stylish lounge features cushy nooks separated by gauzy curtains. *Annankatu 21; 011-358-400-21-1921.*

LISBON Cinco Lounge The cocktail menu at this sophisticated Príncipe Real night spot changes regularly. The current one is organized by era, with each section accompanied by a history lesson. The list runs from "1800–1899" (Cuba Libre) to "1980–2005" (cosmos). *Rua Ruben A. Leitão 17-A; 011-351-21-342-4033; cincolounge.com.*

LONDON 69 Colebrooke Row Tony Conigliaro and two longtime friends run this spunky black and white bar. They use lab equipment to make classic cocktails and creative drinks like the Gonzales: tequila and a honey-water-hydrosol (a water-based essence of the tuberose flower). *69 Colebrooke Row; 011-44-7540-528-593; 69colebrookerow.com.*

LONDON The Bar at the Dorchester Giuliano Morandin has been making stellar classic drinks like the Martinez (Old Tom gin and house-made Boker's bitters) at this London landmark for the past 30 years. World-renowned cocktail authority Harry Craddock was the Dorchester's first head bartender. *53 Park Lane; 011-44-20-7629-8888; thedorchester.com.*

LONDON Connaught Bar Top London bartenders Agostino Perrone and Erik Lorincz created the cocktail list at the recently renovated century-old Connaught Bar. Among the Art Deco bar's new features is a black-leather-topped martini trolley pushed by white-gloved attendants. *Carlos Place; 011-44-20-7499-7070; the-connaught.co.uk.*

LONDON HIX This new Soho restaurant serves Mark Hix's inventive takes on traditional British food. Mark's, the bar downstairs run by Charles Vexenat (creator of El Catador, P. 157), features historic English cocktails such as Gin Punch à la Terrington (gin, green Chartreuse, lemon syrup and soda). *66-70 Brewer St.; 011-44-20-7292-3518; hixsoho.co.uk.*

LONDON Montgomery Place Marian Beke (whose Valencia is on P. 151) works at this softly lit speakeasy serving terrific old-school drinks. *31 Kensington Park Rd.; 011-44-20-7792-3921; montgomeryplace.co.uk.*

LONDON Quo Vadis Club This members-only club in a former home of Karl Marx is on two floors above the excellent British-food destination Quo Vadis. It offers a billiards room, a martini trolley and drinks like Army & Navy (gin, lemon juice and orgeat). *26-29 Dean St.; 011-44-20-7437-9585; quovadissoho.co.uk.*

MADRID Del Diego On a quiet street below the Gran Vía, Fernando del Diego and his two sons operate this breezy bar. It's known for amazing daiquiris as well as drinks like the Diego (vodka, apricot brandy and the brandy-based Bols Advocaat). *Calle de la Reina 12; 011-34-91-523-3106.*

MANCHESTER, ENGLAND Socio Rehab Mixologist Beau Myers runs this small, hard-to-find bar, which has rotating DJs and obscure spirits like triple-distilled Balkan 176° vodka and Del Maguey's Pechuga Single Village mezcal. Guests who have a cocktail club membership get a key to a cabinet of rare spirits. *100 High St.; 011-44-161-832-4529; sociorehab.com.*

MILAN Nottingham Forest At this bar decorated in kitschy greenery, molecular mixologist Dario Comini's unconventional bar arsenal includes dry ice, gold dust and syringes. *Viale Piave 1; 011-39-02-7983-11; nottingham-forest.com.*

MUNICH Negroni With a menu of more than 140 cocktails, 100 whiskies, 40 rums and 40 vodkas, this 12-year-old bar has earned a cult status. Michele Fiordoliva and Mauro Mahjoub serve Italian-inspired dishes and spectacular drinks like the Dusty Martini (gin and apple juice in a Galliano-rinsed glass). *Sedanstrasse 9; 011-49-89-4895-0154; negronibar.de.*

MUNICH Schumann's Bar Bartending legend Charles Schumann, author of the revered *American Bar: The Artistry of Mixing Drinks,* owns this swank see-and-be-seen haunt. The focus is on well-crafted classics (gimlets, martinis), but the bartenders can make virtually any cocktail. *Odeonsplatz 6-7; 011-49-89-2290-60; schumanns.de.*

PARIS Experimental Cocktail Club This neo-Baroque lounge is co-owned by Romée de Goriainoff, who created the recipes in the Brandy chapter (P. 122). True to its name, the bar serves ingenious drinks, like a new-style old-fashioned that's flavored with grapefruit zest. *37 rue St-Sauveur, 2nd Arr.; 011-33-1-4508-8809.*

STOCKHOLM f/l Cocktailbar Run by the owners of the innovative restaurant frantzén/lindeberg across the street, f/l is a bakery by day; at night, it's a supercool members-only bar (although diners from the restaurant can stop in for a drink) led by Jimmy Dymott, creator of the Coffee Brown (P. 160). *Lilla Nygatan 16; 011-46-70-052-4683.*

VIENNA Barfly's Club This cocktail bar in the 19th-century Hotel Fürst Metternich has a menu of 450 drinks, hundreds of rums and whiskeys and a dozen kinds of cigars. *Esterházygasse 33; 011-43-1-586-08-25; barflys.at.*

VIENNA Halbestadt Bar Erich Wassicek oversees the constantly changing list of cocktails at this modish bar in a building designed by late-19th-century Austrian architect Otto Wagner. Occasionally Wassicek invites guests to a private back room—the mixologist's equivalent of a chef's table. *Währinger Gürtel 9; 011-43-1-319-4735; halbestadt.at.*

ZURICH Widder Bar A grand piano and scores of bottles adorn this bar at the Widder Hotel that serves more than 500 spirits—including over 250 single-malt whiskies. Jazz musicians like Roy Hargrove have come to perform. *Rennweg 7; 011-41-44-224-25-26; widderhotel.ch.*

ASIA

HONG KONG Halo This members-only lounge from the team behind the hot spot Volar has a '70s-meets-Victoria look. At the entrance, a face-recognition system searches a database before allowing anyone to enter. *10-12 Stanley St., Central; 011-852-2810-1274; halo.hk.*

OSAKA, JAPAN Bar K For more than a decade, this 16-seat bar has excelled at details like exquisite ice and perfectly executed classic cocktails. *1-3-3 Koyo Bldg., Kita-ku; 011-81-66-343-1167.*

SHANGHAI Chinatown This three-story club conjures a Hollywood version of 1930s Shanghai, with showgirls and Chinese acrobats. Bartender C.J. Wang uses hand-chipped double-frozen ice at the VIP Observatory Bar. *471 Zhapu Rd.; 011-86-21-6258-2078.*

SHANGHAI Constellation 2 This outpost of tiny cocktail lounge Constellation serves the same stellar drinks as the original but has two floors and an updated gentlemen's club look. The 350 single-malt whiskies can be ordered with slices of Italian ham or Chinese melon alongside. *33 Yongjia Rd.; 011-86-21-5465-5993.*

SINGAPORE Tippling Club Chef Ryan Clift and mixologist Matthew Bax are behind this temple of molecular gastronomy and mixology. The spirit selection is incredible, as are drinks like Pharmacy, a pill bottle filled with gin and accompanied by a Campari-filled syringe and a fizzy citrus-syrup capsule. *8D Dempsey Rd.; 011-65-6475-2217; tipplingclub.com.*

TOKYO Bar High Five Owner Hidetsugu Ueno, contributor of the Classics chapter (P. 26), trained at Tokyo's

top 100 bars worldwide

legendary Star Bar Ginza. His signature White Lady is an outstanding gin-based sidecar; other mixologists say it's the best drink they've ever had. *Polestar Bldg. 26, 7-2-14 Ginza, Chuo-ku; 011-81-3-3571-5815.*

TOKYO Star Bar Ginza
Mentor to Bar High Five's Hidetsugu Ueno, Hisashi Kishi offers exquisitely made cocktails and a top-quality Scotch selection at this legendary basement bar. *Sankosha Bldg., 1-5-13 Ginza, Chuo-ku; 011-81-3-3535-8005.*

TOKYO Tender Bar
Master bartender Kazuo Uyeda—inventor of the "hard shake"—owns Tender Bar, where he and his assistant bartenders craft meticulous cocktails with premium handpicked spirits. *Nogakudo Bldg., 6-5-15 Ginza, Chuo-ku; 011-81-3-3571-8343.*

AUSTRALIA

BRISBANE The Bowery
Named after the New York City street famous during Prohibition for its speakeasies, Bowery offers live jazz, a huge whisky selection and drinks like the Grand Affair (limited-release Hedonism whisky, Grand Marnier and kaffir lime). *676 Ann St.; 011-61-7-3252-0202; thebowery. com.au/home.html.*

BRISBANE Lark
This restaurant and bar is owned by Perry Scott, who trained under Dale DeGroff at New York City's Rainbow Room. Drinks are categorized as "Prelude," "Body" or "Epilogue" (before, during and after dinner). The Jackrabbit Slim (Calvados and quince liqueur) is a Prelude drink. *1/267 Given Terrace; 011-61-7-3369-1299; thelark.com.au.*

MELBOURNE Black Pearl
Distressed wood floors and old velvet couches belie the fantastic cocktails here. Bartenders Cristiano Berretto, Chris Hysted and Greg Sanderson present their creations in vintage crystal glasses. *304 Brunswick St.; 011-61-3-9417-0455.*

MELBOURNE Der Raum
From star mixologist Matthew Bax, the detail-obsessed Der Raum (pronounced "dare-rawm") makes its own Boker's bitters using an 1800s recipe. Drinks range from old-school classics to the modern Smokey Old Bastard, made with "citrus smoke." *438 Church St.; 011-61-3-9428-0055; derraum.com.au.*

MELBOURNE Eighteen-O-Six (1806)
Sebastian Reaburn, creator of the Mocktails chapter (P. 162), runs this velvet curtain–framed bar. The menu follows a time line from the 1700s to the present and has historical information on

each drink. The Whiskey Bang (whiskey, hard cider, honey and spices) is based on a recipe from the 1860 book *The Practical Housewife. 169 Exhibition St.; 011-61-3-9663-7722; 1806.com.au.*

MELBOURNE Golden Monkey The ambience here is fantastic (the lounge is designed to look like a 1920s opium den), and so are the Asian-inspired tapas and creative cocktails. The Sleeping Dragon (Cognac, bourbon and walnut syrup) is served in a fig water–spritzed tumbler. *389 Lonsdale St.; 011-61-3-9602-2055; goldenmonkey.com.au.*

MELBOURNE Seamstress This four-story Cantonese-inflected restaurant has two bars and exceptional updated classics by Jason Chan, who created the citrusy Commodore 64 (P. 158). *113 Lonsdale St.; 011-61-3-9663-6363; seamstress.com.au.*

SYDNEY Ivy Bar This open-air bar in Sydney's huge, superchic Merivale shopping and nightlife center features inspired drinks like the Secret Garden (tequila, basil, cucumber). Upstairs, Ivy Lounge is an elegant take on a 1950s tropical lounge. *330 George St.; 011-61-2-9240-3000.*

SYDNEY Rockpool Bar & Grill Neil Perry's new outpost of his Melbourne steak house has a '50s-era drink menu from Linden Pride (who created the Tiger on P. 160). Cocktails like Moscow Mules—vodka, fresh ginger and house-made ginger beer—pair well with bar food like the bacon wagyu burger. *66 Hunter St.; 011-61-2-8078-1900; rockpool.com.*

NEW ZEALAND

WELLINGTON Matterhorn Originally owned by two Swiss brothers, this bar now has late-night music and handcrafted drinks. The Fig & Cigar French

75 is made with Cognac, Champagne and fig-and-cigar-syrup (infused with actual cigar). *106 Cuba St.; 011-64-4-384-3359; matterhorn.co.nz.*

WELLINGTON Motel Bar The '50s-esque bar has a new themed menu every six months: "Smugglers & Highwaymen" has drinks like Bootlegger's Breakfast (whiskey, marmalade, lemon juice and chicory) and cigars. *Door 2, Forresters Lane; 011-64-4-384-9084.*

AFRICA

CAPE TOWN Bascule Whisky, Wine and Cocktail Bar This bar inside the waterfront Cape Grace Hotel has over 400 whiskies from nearly every whisky-producing region in the world. Whisky Club members receive personalized cut-crystal whisky tumblers. *W. Quay Rd., Victoria and Alfred Waterfront; 011-27-21-410-7238.*

the food guide

These restaurants and cocktail spots provided the delicious, drink-friendly recipes for our Party Food chapter (p. 176).

Alibi Room
12236 W. Washington Blvd., Los Angeles
310-390-9300
alibiroomla.com

Bar 228
Le Meurice
228 rue de Rivoli
1st Arr., Paris
011-33-1-4458-1066

Café de la Concha
Paseo de la Concha
San Sebastián, Spain
011-34-943-473-600

Chinawhite
4 Winsley St., London
011-44-20-7291-1480

Cole's
118 E. Sixth St.
Los Angeles
213-622-4090
colesfrenchdip.com

The Corner Suite Bistro De Luxe
850 Thurlow St.
Vancouver
604-569-3415
thecornersuite.com

D-Heartman
Miyukikan Bldg., 4F
6-5-17 Ginza, Chuo-ku
Tokyo
011-81-3-3573-6123

The East Room
2A Tabernacle St.
London
011-44-20-7065-6842
thstrm.com

Gran Bar Danzon
Libertad 1161
Buenos Aires
011-54-11-4811-1108

Ketsi
Four Seasons Resort
Punta Mita, Mexico
011-52-329-291-6000

Le Bar du Plaza Athénée
25 av. Montaigne
8th Arr., Paris
011-33-1-5367-6600

Mesa & Manifesto
748 Julu Rd.
Shanghai
011-86-21-6289-9108
mesa-manifesto.com

Minetta Tavern
133 MacDougal St.
212-475-3850
minettatavernny.com

Momofuku Ssäm Bar
207 Second Ave.
Manhattan
212-254-3500
momofuku.com

New York Bar
Park Hyatt Tokyo
3-7-1-2 Nishi-Shinjuku
Shinjuku-ku, Tokyo
011-81-3-5322-1234

The Parrot Club
363 Fortaleza St.
San Juan, Puerto Rico
787-725-7370
oofrestaurants.com

Proof on Main
702 W. Main St.
Louisville, KY
502-217-6360
proofonmain.com

Seamstress
113 Lonsdale St.
Melbourne
011-61-3-9663-6363
seamstress.com.au

Spice Temple
10 Bligh St.
Sydney
011-61-2-8078-1888
rockpool.com.au

barware guide

218

RUM

P. 96 "Stockholm" tumbler by Giarimi, huset-shop.com. **P. 97** "Alto" Champagne saucer, calvinklein.com; flute by Roost, swallowglass.com. **P. 103** "Palm" pitcher by Giarimi, huset-shop.com; "Sprigs" glass by Artel, tableartonline.com. **P. 107** "Mitos" coupe by Květná, ameico.com.

WHISKEY

P. 108 Bowl, moserusa.com. **P. 109** "Mitos" glass by Květná, ameico.com; "Patrician" Champagne cup by Lobmeyr, neuegalerie.org; "Kikatsu" glass by Kimura Glass Co., easternaccent.com. **P. 113** "Essence" cocktail glass by Alfredo Häberli, iittala.com. **P. 117** Champagne glass by Peter Behrens, ameico.com. **P. 121** "Drift Ice" glass, moserusa.com.

BRANDY

P. 122 Tumblers by Roost, swallowglass.com. **P. 123** "Rose Stem" swizzle sticks by Laura Walls Taylor, etsy.com/shop/laurawallstaylor. **P. 127** "Silver Band" flute by Dorothy C. Thorpe, replacements.com; "Lulu" decanter, williamyeowardcrystal.com. **P. 131** "Whisky" glass, moserusa.com.

PUNCHES

P. 134 Punch cups, crateandbarrel.com. **P. 135** "Silver Band" punch bowl by Dorothy C. Thorpe, replacements.com. **P. 139** "Bamboo" tumbler by Roost, velocityartanddesign.com. **P. 141** "Lulu" ice bucket and "Caroline" tumbler, williamyeowardcrystal.com.

P. 145 Punch bowl and glasses by Nasonmoretti from Seguso, 212-696-1133.

MIXOLOGIST ALL-STARS

P. 149 "Bark" cocktail shaker by Roost, nestinteriorsny.com; "Patrician" Champagne cup by Lobmeyr, neuegalerie.org. **P. 155** "Library Stripe" tumblers by Kate Spade, lenox.com. **P. 159** "Vesta" double old-fashioned tumbler, williamyeowardcrystal.com.

MOCKTAILS

P. 163 "Gold Band" martini glass by Dorothy C. Thorpe, replacements.com; "Pebbles" highball glass, moserusa.com. **P. 167** "Golden Leaf Aliseo" glass by Nasonmoretti from Seguso, 212-696-1133; brass cocktail pick, hausinterior.com. **P. 171** "Ottagonale" highball glasses by Carlo Moretti, tableartonline.com.

PARTY FOOD

PP. 176–177 "Basso" plates, calvinklein.com; napkins, paperproductsdesign.com; glass, nouvelstudio.com. **P. 181** "Loos" glass by Lobmeyr, neuegalerie.org. **P. 187** Tray by Two's Company, globaltable.com. **P. 189** "Float" bowl by Molo, velocityartanddesign.com. **P. 191** "Ripple" plate by Urban Oasis from ABC Home, 212-473-3000. **P. 195** "Verona" glass, nouvelstudio.com. **P. 199** Glass, nouvelstudio.com.

recipe index

PAGE NUMBERS IN **BOLD** INDICATE PHOTOGRAPHS.

recipe index

PAGE NUMBERS IN **BOLD** INDICATE PHOTOGRAPHS.

thank you

This collection of cocktails would not have
been possible without the help of these people.

Melanie Asher, Greg Boehm, Cameron Bogue,
Jamie Boudreau, Jacob Briars, Anamaria
Ceseña, Alex Day, Simon Ford, Rob Fuentevilla,
John Gakuru, Jessica Gonzalez, Rob McKeown,
Valerie Meehan, Junior Merino, Brian Miller,
Kevin Patricio, Thomas Waugh and Rhea Wong

More books from
FOOD&WINE

Best of the Best
Cookbook Recipes
The best recipes from the
25 best cookbooks of the year

Annual Cookbook 2010
An entire year of recipes from
FOOD & WINE Magazine

Wine Guide 2010
The most up-to-date guide, with
more than 1,000 recommendations

Available wherever books are
sold, or call 800-284-4145
or log on to foodandwine.com/books.